THE BATTLE OF WHITE PLAINS

THE BATTLE OF
WHITE PLAINS

Washington and Howe in Westchester

STEPHEN PAUL DeVILLO

THE
History
PRESS

Published by The History Press
Charleston, SC
www.historypress.com

Copyright © 2022 by Stephen Paul DeVillo
All rights reserved

Cover illustration: The Delaware Regiment at Chatterton Hill. *Painting by George Albert Harker, courtesy of the Westchester County Historical Society.*

First published 2022

ISBN 978-1-5402-5269-2

Library of Congress Control Number: 2022933362

Notice: The information in this book is true and complete to the best of our knowledge. It is offered without guarantee on the part of the author or The History Press. The author and The History Press disclaim all liability in connection with the use of this book.

*Respectfully dedicated to the men and women
of the Brigade of the American Revolution.*

CONTENTS

ACKNOWLEDGEMENTS

I t takes a small army to write a book, and I am grateful to the many people who have given me support, encouragement, information and insights. My special thanks to:

My mother, Patricia Edwards Clyne, for the use of her Westchester County book collection.

Frank Clyne, whose shared enthusiasm for geology and minerology informed my understanding of terrain and how landforms came to be where they are.

Jane Williams, who has often accompanied me on various excursions in search of history.

The East Bronx History Forum, the Kingsbridge Historical Society and their dedicated corps of Bronx historians who contributed information and insights: Thomas X. Casey, Tom Vasti, Nick Dembowski, Nicholas DiBrino, Kevin Graham, Mike Gupta, Angel Hernandez, Peter Ostrander, Nilka Martell, Jorge Santiago, Rich Vitacco and Toby Z. Liederman of the Hutchinson River Restoration Project.

Blake Bell, Pelham town historian, whose detailed research into the history of Pelham Manor shed new light on the Battle of Pell's Point.

Richard Forliano, Eastchester town historian, for his support and insights.

Michael Virgintino for helping locate the American entrenchments on Mount Misery.

Dr. Eric Sanderson for his research into the environment of Manhattan and the Bronx.

David Osborne, site manager of the St. Paul's Church National Historic Site, for his walking tours of the Pell's Point battlefield.

The Reverend Jeffrey Geary for his research into White Plains's history.

Howard and Lea Waldman, battlefield residents and fellow Bronx River Ramblers, for their enthusiasm and support.

Michael Grillo, who, as His Excellency General Washington, has been indefatigable in bringing history to life.

Cynthia Kauffman and Debra Palazzo of the Daughters of Liberty's Legacy for their unstinting support for commemorating the history of White Plains and the Revolutionary War in Westchester.

Tom and Marianne Tucker of Tucker's Tales Puppet Theater, who, at the Battle of Trenton commemorations and other venues, put on *The Trouble with Trenton*, a uniquely enjoyable and educational historical outdoor puppet show.

Particular thanks go to the Bronx River Alliance for its sponsorship of the Bronx River Rambles walking tours that helped focus my research and knowledge of the Bronx River and to the Westchester chapter of the American Association of University Women, which has hosted me in giving historical talks that helped hone my research.

A number of local organizations deserve gratitude for their dedicated efforts to preserve history: the Bronx County Historical Society, the Dobbs Ferry Historical Society, the Eastchester Historical Society, the Friends of the Miller House, the Friends of the Odell House Rochambeau Headquarters, the National Society of Colonial Dames in the State of New York, the North Castle Historical Society, the Old Stone House Museum, the Scarsdale Historical Society, the Van Cortlandt House Museum, the Westchester Historical Society, the White Plains Historical Society and the Yonkers Historical Society.

Additional thanks to the Green-Wood Cemetery for its annual commemoration of the Battle of Brooklyn and to the Trenton Downtown Association and the Old Barracks Museum for their annual sponsorship of the Patriots Week commemorations and reenactments of the Battles of Trenton.

Lastly, hats off and a hearty "huzzah" to the Brigade of the American Revolution and, in particular, to the men and women of the Second and Fifth New York Regiments, whose dedicated participation in numerous reenactment events in the New York area make history "real" in ways books alone cannot achieve.

Introduction

We commemorate 1776 as the year of independence, but it was also the year that independence was nearly lost. The small crossroads village of White Plains in central Westchester County, New York, was one of the places the war might have ended in defeat for the American cause.

The Battle of White Plains is often given short shrift in accounts of the Revolutionary War, passed over as a mere interval between the disastrous Battle of Brooklyn and the desperate "retreat to victory" that ended in the Battles of Trenton and Princeton. The ambiguity of the battle's outcome belies its importance. White Plains was neither a stunning victory nor a calamitous defeat; rather, it was a prolonged standoff between an aggressive American general pressed onto the defensive and a British general who was reluctant to attack. Nevertheless, the hills of central Westchester during that last week of October 1776 witnessed the end point of a campaign that had seen repeated opportunities for the British to trap and destroy George Washington's ragtag army and end the newborn quest for American independence.

The Battle of White Plains was a critical episode in a campaign shaped by luck and misfortune, valor and caution, resolution and pusillanimity, good weather and high water. The battle's outcome was brought about by actions and decisions that were not always fully informed nor well advised. It was fought by men with imperfect knowledge of the enemy's strength and intentions—and even of the landscape they were contesting. For the

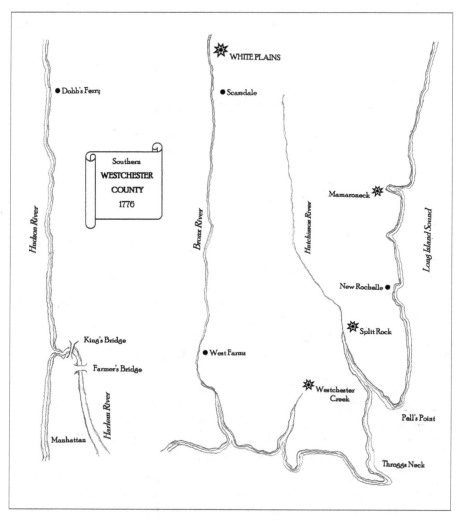

Map 1: Southern Westchester County, 1776. *Map by author.*

British, the battle was a fading chance to terminate the fledgling army of the newly independent United States. For the bedraggled Americans, outmaneuvered in a string of defeats, White Plains was a place to take a stand and secure a path to temporary safety, from which they would continue the struggle.

Chapter 1

RETREAT FROM BROOKLYN

The 1776 campaign season began on a note of triumph when the British pulled out of Boston on March 17, ending an eleven-month siege and yielding a victory to George Washington and the new Continental army. Watching the last British sail vanish over the horizon, American observers had no illusions that the war was over. The empire would surely strike back, and the Crown forces withdrew to Halifax, Nova Scotia, for rest, refit and reinforcement while they planned the reconquest of the thirteen colonies.

Studying the map, Washington deduced that the port city of New York was the likeliest place where King George's soldiers would launch their comeback, and he marched his army down from Boston to defend it. He did not have long to wait. By the time the Declaration of Independence was read out to the assembled troops on July 9, the first wave of British troops had arrived and occupied Staten Island, awaiting the arrival of a much larger fleet that would bring their field army to thirty-two thousand, under the command of General William Howe.

Things quickly went downhill from there. At the Battle of Brooklyn on August 27, the Americans suffered catastrophic losses of dead, wounded and captured, but thanks to the heroic efforts of the Maryland and Delaware Regiments, a substantial proportion of the army escaped the converging enemy forces and got to the entrenchments covering downtown Brooklyn. The Americans were now hemmed in against the East River, but the British lost the opportunity to destroy the trapped army when, two days later,

Washington carried out a daring midnight withdrawal across the river to Manhattan. The Battle of Brooklyn would mark the beginning of a pattern of fumbled initiatives that would characterize the British effort for the rest of the year.

Hesitancy was the hallmark of William Howe's generalship. After the Battle of Brooklyn, he waited two full weeks before making his move on Manhattan Island. By then, Washington had concluded that with the Royal Navy controlling the surrounding waters, he could not defend New York City, and he had begun shifting his forces to the high ground on the northern end of the island. When the British finally landed on the middle of the island on September 15, they quickly put the opposing militia to flight, but their slow advance and the hasty retreat of the remaining American troops in the city again robbed Howe of the chance to corner the rebel army.

A dejected America slumps in despair amid news of British victories. British optimism in the summer of 1776 would prove to be premature. *Library of Congress.*

The next day, a chance skirmish and an incautious British response resulted in the morale-boosting American victory at the Battle of Harlem Heights. Though of little strategic consequence, the Harlem Heights affray would redouble Howe's caution and influence his actions in the weeks to come.

British officers would often belittle the rough farmer-soldiers in Washington's army, but the once-aggressive Howe had learned the hard way not to underestimate them. Before being appointed commander in chief, Howe had been the ground commander at the assault on Bunker Hill on June 17, 1775, a sanguinary battle in which the British had carried the day but at a cost of nearly one thousand dead and wounded, one-quarter of the attacking force. Howe himself had come through unharmed but saw every man in his entourage hit. Profoundly shaken by the experience, Howe would never again take a cavalier attitude toward the embattled rebel farmers.

Popular memory of the Revolutionary War envisions overladen redcoats directed by stodgy generals as they maneuvered in inappropriately rigid battle formations. Howe, though, was far from stodgy or tradition-bound. Familiar with conditions in America, Howe in fact had actively promoted the organization and training of "light infantry," lightly burdened soldiers trained to maneuver in loose, open order as they took to the woods and fought over uneven ground. Howe's timorous approach was thus not due to unfamiliarity with America or to rigid traditionalism; rather, it was due to the aptitude with which Americans dug fortifications and the ruthlessness with which they poured fire on advancing attackers.

Howe's cautious approach may also be explained by his role as a peace commissioner, empowered, along with his brother Admiral Richard Howe, to end the rebellion by negotiation. His brother Richard had, in fact, convened his own peace conference a week before the British landed in Manhattan, meeting at the southern tip of Staten Island with Benjamin Franklin, John Adams and Edward Rutledge. The peace conference was a nonstarter once the American delegation made it clear that independence was nonnegotiable.

Disappointed but not altogether surprised by the outcome of the peace conference, William Howe nevertheless may have hoped that by keeping up pressure on the rebel army, the revolution would collapse of its own accord with minimal battle casualties. One thing that Howe knew for certain was that his army could not suffer any more losses on the scale of Bunker Hill. His well-trained redcoats were not easily replaced; it took up to three years to turn a raw recruit into a fully fledged regular, and in any event, few men in Britain or Ireland were stepping forward to enlist for the war in America. The British army had never been large to begin with and had an expanding empire to defend and police, prompting the government to hire units of foreign auxiliaries—or, in other words, the Hessians.

This was not the first time Britain had called on the Hessians. Brunswick and Hesse-Cassel, among others, had provided troops as Britain's allies in the Seven Years' War (1756–63), and Hessian auxiliaries had helped suppress revolts in Scotland and Ireland. Britain was not unique in hiring foreign auxiliaries; international law of the time considered the practice legitimate.

The Hessians would play a major role in the campaigns of 1776, but it is unfair to term them mercenaries. Though their ranks may have included a few footloose soldiers of fortune, Hessian regiments were hired out by their respective lords and monarchs. Germany, at this time, was divided into some three hundred separate political entities, ranging from the substantial kingdoms of Prussia and Bavaria to a bewildering array of small duchies,

RECRUITS.

British army recruiters found few recruits willing to sign on to fight in America, prompting the government to hire foreign auxiliaries. *Library of Congress.*

principalities, electorates and palatinates. Looking for trained soldiers for the American war, British agents sought out cash-strapped mini-monarchs with regiments for rent.

Prominent among these minor-league autocrats was Frederick II, Landgrave of Hesse-Cassel, a son-in-law of the late King George II. A military enthusiast who modeled his regiments on the army of his namesake, Frederick the Great, he would supply twelve thousand of the thirty thousand

German troops in the British service, giving them their enduring nickname of "Hessians." Other German units hailed from a tongue-twisting array of places: Hesse-Hanau, Waldeck, Brunswick, Ansbach-Bayreuth and Anhalt-Zerbst.

Individual soldiers had no say in the matter. Many of them were conscripts snatched out of taverns or nabbed at the crossroads to bring the regiments up to strength. Some thirty thousand Hessians would eventually serve in America and elsewhere; several thousand would desert and remain in America after the war, converting themselves from hated invaders to valued immigrants.

However impressive they were in numbers, the British forces in America that summer of 1776 were a divided army. Converging on New York from separate ports in England and Germany, the British and Hessians were like a couple whose first date was their wedding day. There had been no time for the sort of joint staff exercises or combined training maneuvers that would meld the two disparate nationalities into a smoothly functioning allied command.

Language was a big part of the problem. For all the planning that had gone into assembling and dispatching the Hessian forces, no one, it seems, had thought about providing interpreters. Perhaps it was assumed that educated officers could converse in French if need be, but when the aged Hessian senior commander Leopold Philip de Heister presented himself to General Howe, he found that he had no common language with the monolingual Englishman.[1] Another Hessian officer, Levin von Münchhausen, was eventually detailed to serve as interpreter, but things did not go smoothly. Howe disliked de Heister from the outset, and Münchhausen's heel-clicking continental formality annoyed him, but for the time being, the three men were stuck with one another.

Relations among the lower ranks were little better. With unit pride fostered by long-term enlistments, the proud British redcoats tended to look down on everyone else as poseurs or wannabees. Somewhat resentful of these blue-coated foreigners with their funny waxed moustaches and long queues, they were dismissive of the Hessians as a bunch of dumb sheep and wondered how reliable they would prove to be in battle. Army quartermasters soon learned to keep British and Hessian bivouacs well apart from each other to avoid the inevitable fistfights.

The redcoats and their officers had even less regard for American Loyalists seeking to serve their king by enlisting in volunteer units. The redcoats' "leave it to us professionals" attitude probably hampered the chances for British success early in the war. The army did little to attract Loyalists, and Loyalist units (often raised by local landowners) were generally shunted to one side. Nor were enslaved Blacks recruited at this time; despite the proclamation of royal governor Dunmore in Virginia, Howe's official policy would not embrace recruiting Black Loyalists until 1777. Later British commanders would increasingly come to rely on Loyalist units, but for the most part, they would deny them the right to wear the royal red livery, leaving them to be uniformed in green or brown instead.

This motley coalition of Crown forces was now poised to invade the mainland and decide the fate of the nascent American nation.

Chapter 2

FRUSTRATION AT FROG'S NECK

After the Battle of Harlem Heights, Howe left the defiant rebels to glare down from their upper Manhattan fortifications and did what he did best, calling another pause while he sorted his troops out and consolidated his occupation of New York City and Long Island. Campaigns in the eighteenth century were customarily conducted at a deliberate pace, and an eighteenth-century gentleman such as Howe never allowed himself to be rushed or hurried. He had thus far conducted a victorious campaign at a reasonably low cost in British dead and wounded, and there was no need to make any hasty decisions. The affair at Harlem Heights, though, had cost the British more than 140 casualties, too high a price to pay for such a pointless tussle, and it showed that the entrenched Americans were still a force to be reckoned with.

Settling down with his staff in a house on Bowling Green at the southern tip of Manhattan, Howe spent nearly a month devising a new strategy for dealing with Washington. Part of the reason for the delay was that he was hoping for the arrival of a contingent of six thousand British and Hessian reinforcements, which he understood had already sailed from Portsmouth, England. Embarkation, though, did not mean there was a reliable timeline for arrival. Bucking prevailing westerly winds and the Gulf Stream, east to west Atlantic crossings could take an inordinate amount of time, as much as ten weeks or more even in good weather. As the days stretched into weeks without reinforcements, Howe reluctantly concluded that he would have to go ahead with the forces he had on hand.

A morale-boosting American victory at Harlem Heights showed that the rebel army was far from defeated. *Library of Congress.*

Among these forces, Howe's strongest card was the Royal Navy, which controlled the waters of New York Harbor and the Hudson estuary and which, in theory, could transport and land British soldiers anywhere in the New York archipelago.

Glancing at the ship masts crowding the harbor, Howe's second-in-command, Henry Clinton, pushed for a landing at the northern tip of Manhattan or on the southern shore of the adjacent mainland to seize the bridges leading off the island. This would bottle the rebel army in Harlem Heights, where, caught between two converging forces with no escape route, it would surely go down in defeat, effectively snuffing out the rebellion.

Looking at the map, this idea seemed to make perfect sense, but the local geography posed impediments that not even the Royal Navy could overcome. While William Howe and Henry Clinton were focused on the land areas, Admiral Richard Howe possessed detailed nautical charts that told him a different story. The shoreline of the Hudson River along upper Manhattan was for the most part rocky with a steep drop-off and thus presented no places where a significant force could be safely landed. The Hudson estuary being a glacial fjord, this situation extended to the shoreline of the mainland, with the added obstacle of a steep ridge between the Hudson River's shoreline and the Kings Bridge. Marshes, mud flats and contending tidal surges likewise made Spuyten Duyvil Creek, between Manhattan and the mainland, difficult for even small craft.

A small force might be stealthily landed, which in itself could be sufficient to seize and hold the mainland bridgeheads, but American forces at Fort Independence and other outposts would interdict and overpower any small force coming ashore. Well aware of the vulnerability of the Harlem River bridgeheads, the Americans had placed fortifications along the high ground overlooking them. Recognizing their importance, Washington had taken the trouble to personally inspect them; at the site of one of the outposts, Fort No. 4, locals would later point to an indentation in the bedrock as "Washington's footprint."

Shying away from a direct assault against Harlem Heights from the south and unable to land a major force in the north, William Howe's next move would instead follow a well-worn page from his tactical playbook: a wide flanking maneuver, this time to the eastern shore of the present-day Bronx. Unlike the rocky shores of the Hudson River and Spuyten Duyvil, the shoreline along Long Island Sound was a glacial outwash plain and thus offered a variety of smooth landing places, presumably far enough out to be free of interfering rebel units and providing fairly even terrain from there to the Kings Bridge. If Howe could land a significant expeditionary force, quickly march a few miles westward and bypass or neutralize the American forts, he could seize the only two bridges that connected Manhattan with the mainland, leaving Washington nowhere to go.[2]

The only drawback to this option was having to navigate the notorious Hell Gate. The well-named Hell Gate on the East River lay about halfway between the docks of lower Manhattan and Howe's destination on the shore

Defeated at Brooklyn and Kip's Bay, Washington, here depicted on the Princeton battle memorial, was forced to abandon New York City. *Photo by author.*

of Long Island Sound. A treacherous confluence of opposing tidal surges underlain with hull-tearing rocks, Hell Gate was a notorious ship graveyard, and it would require careful timing, along with precision depth sounding and knowledge of the tide tables, to get a fleet through without mishap.

After a spell of wet, stormy weather delayed the expedition to October 12, Admiral Richard Howe's seamanship got the invasion fleet through intact, though Hell Gate nevertheless exacted its toll when three artillerymen were lost from an overturned boat.

Past Hell Gate, the shore of southern Westchester tended to be either rocky or marshy for the first few miles, but reaching down into Long Island Sound, the peninsula of Throggs Neck (then commonly called Frog's Neck) held out an inviting hand to Howe's flotilla. It lay almost due east from the Kings Bridge crossings, and a road ran from the peninsula through Westchester Town and West Farms, offering a straight line of march of about seven miles to Kings Bridge. Throggs Neck also offered a sheltered bay on its western side, with a sandy landing beach a stone's throw from the eastern end of the road to Westchester Town.

Throggs Neck, though, was more of an island than a peninsula, cut off from the mainland by salt marshes and Westchester Creek. A tidal estuary, Westchester Creek had a deep channel lined by gooey mud banks that confined foot crossing to a long causeway and a wooden bridge. North of the bridge, the creek broadened into a millpond, and fording points beyond that were concealed by still more trackless salt marshes.[3]

The American general William Heath, tasked with keeping watch over possible landing sites along the Sound, had posted Colonel Edward Hand and twenty-five of his Pennsylvania riflemen at Throggs Neck. Upon the approach of the British invasion flotilla, they promptly withdrew across the creek, pulled up the planks of the bridge behind them and calmly sighted their rifles.

Unlike the standard smoothbore musket, a rifle had its barrel grooved on the inside to give the ball a spin as it exited, thereby increasing its range and accuracy (using the same principle as when throwing a football). But to enable the round leaden bullet to catch the grooves, a very tight fit was necessary when loading, reducing the rifle's rate of fire to one bullet a minute versus three for a musket, leaving riflemen vulnerable to a bayonet assault while they laboriously reloaded. Rifles had gunsights, though, unlike infantry muskets. In trained hands, a rifle could be precisely targeted and kill at two hundred yards or more, instead of a musket's effective range of fifty to seventy-five yards. Safe from bayonet attacks on the far side of Westchester Creek, Hand's men could take their time and pick off their enemies one by one.

Howe's men arrived at Westchester Creek only to find themselves stopped by a torn-up bridge and a fusillade of well-aimed shots from those deadly Pennsylvania rifles. By evening, Heath had reinforced the riflemen with

Left: Pennsylvania riflemen stymied Howe's crossing at Westchester Creek, preventing the British advance to Kingsbridge. *Photo by author.*

Right: British general William Howe's cautious pursuit of the campaign frustrated his subordinates and wasted opportunities for a decisive victory. *Library of Congress.*

1,200 troops and positioned a cannon to cover the bridge and blast anyone foolish enough to try to tiptoe across the bare beams. Unable to locate an alternate route across the creek, Howe was stymied, and in typical form, he called a halt to reconsider his options.

At this point, General Charles Lee arrived at Washington's headquarters. Fresh from overseeing the defeat of a British assault on Charles Town, South Carolina, Lee was about to urge Washington to reconsider *his* options. Second-in-command of the fledgling American army, Lee's career included service as an officer in the British regulars, as well as a stint as a European soldier of fortune. His outspoken political opinions had gotten him blackballed from further promotion in the British army, so after immigrating to America in 1773, at the outbreak of the Revolution, he offered his services to the rebels. Off-putting and rather full of himself, he was quick to offer his advice to Washington, and Washington, respectful of Lee's wide-ranging combat experience, usually listened.

Washington, of course, knew of Howe's Throggs Neck landing but did not seem unduly alarmed by the danger such a maneuver could pose. Reluctant to relinquish his grip on Manhattan Island, he had nevertheless begun to shift some units to the high ground on the mainland, but he still kept his main force entrenched in northern Manhattan.

Lee, though, could see clearly that a British expedition, striking west from a landing on the Sound, could quickly interdict the Harlem River crossings and leave Washington trapped on the island. General Heath concurred, pointing out that although Howe was, for the moment, stalled on Throggs Neck, he would sooner or later find himself a better landing place. An American council of war consequently agreed to a pullout from Manhattan, leaving behind only the three-thousand-man garrison of Fort Washington to deny Britain's complete control of the island.

Meanwhile, Howe dithered. If nothing else, Throggs Neck was an agreeable place for the men to camp out. They could pitch their tents in level fields lining the road, and three freshwater springs kept men and horses well hydrated. Moreover, the same impediments that blocked his advance also sheltered his force from rebel incursions. Ensconced in such comfortable circumstances, Howe spent six days on Throggs Neck before deciding on a new landing place at Pell's Point, a few miles up the coast. After a short sail, Howe's men came ashore at Pell's Point on October 18—the same day that Washington was completing his withdrawal from Harlem Heights—heading to a new point of concentration on Valentine's Hill on the mainland.

Chapter 3

THE BATTLE OF PELL'S POINT

Named for a local Dutch farming family, Valentine's (or Volentine's) Hill is a long ridge connecting the present-day Bronx with Yonkers. Though the area was mostly part of the manor of the Loyalist Frederick Philipse III, whose mansion sat by the Hudson River on the west side of the ridge, the inhabitants of the freehold enclave of Mile Square on the east side were rebel friendly and a good source of information and guides.

Many of Philipse's tenant farmers were pro-independence as well, such as Thomas Sherwood, whose house still stands by the Tuckahoe Road and who risked the ire of his landlord to serve in the New York Militia. Memory of Washington's passage would linger in the area's local lore; for years after, a somewhat tent-shaped rock shelter (long demolished) on Park Hill in Yonkers would be dubbed Washington's Cave, though it is unlikely Washington ever used it. Forming part of the western side of the Bronx River valley, Valentine's Hill offered good defensive terrain while pointing a route to the central part of Westchester County, with the Bronx River providing flank protection. And central Westchester was where Washington needed to go.

Washington's plan was to lead his diminished army north to the safety of the rugged Hudson Highlands, where the harsh terrain would hopefully shelter it for the time being. First, though, he would have to stop at the crossroads town of White Plains on the east side of the Bronx River. With

The modest span of the King's Bridge over Spuyten Duyvil Creek was Washington's line of retreat off Manhattan Island. *Benson Lossing,* Pictorial Field Book of the Revolution.

VIEW AT KING'S BRIDGE.

British forces gathering on the eastern shore of Westchester, this was a risky move, but White Plains was where newly arrived supplies of pork and flour from Connecticut were stored, supplies that Washington could not afford to lose. Before he could bring his battered army into the fastness of the Hudson Highlands, Washington needed to secure those supplies and hold White Plains long enough to get the slow-moving wagons well on their way north to the depot at Fishkill.

With local maps sketchy at best, the route to White Plains from Valentine's Hill was far from certain. Taking the York Road (present-day White Plains Road/Post Road) that ran up the eastern side of the Bronx River would offer too tempting a target for British forces striking inland from the Sound, so Washington needed a route that would keep the Bronx River between him and Howe while staying clear of British warships on the Hudson.

In a countryside known to be infested with Loyalists, it was risky to ask for directions, as any local guide beyond Yonkers could turn out to be a Tory spy or double agent. Washington instead dispatched Colonel Rufus Putnam to scout out a secure route. While it seemed odd to dispatch a colonel on a scouting mission, Rufus, the son of Washington's division commander Israel Putnam, was the chief engineer of the Continental army. As an engineer, Putnam could be depended on to have a discerning eye for terrain and to distinguish a farm lane from a roadway good enough to send an army along. Carefully avoiding British patrols and stray Tories, Putnam probed his way up the valley, crossing the river and going as far north as the present-day Wayside Cottage in Scarsdale.

Concluding that the York Road on the east bank of the river was indeed too risky, Putnam eventually found a usable route leading north from Tuckahoe on the west bank of the river. An old Native American path led down from Valentine's Hill to Tuckahoe; to prepare for his northward movement, Washington ordered a hasty widening of this path (the present-day Tuckahoe Road) in order to get his troops and wagons down to the Bronx River and thence north to White Plains. (Part of the road to White Plains exists today as Old Army Road.)

Rufus Putnam's reconnaissance went as far as the present-day Wayside Cottage in Scarsdale. Concluding that the York Road was too risky, he sought out an alternate route to White Plains west of the Bronx River. *Photo by author.*

In the meantime, Howe's rowboats had scraped the sand at Pell's Point just as the last of Washington's wagons rumbled across the Kings Bridge (paying no tolls to the bridge's Loyalist owner, Frederick Philipse III). Now known as Rodman's Neck, Pell's Point sheltered Turtle Cove on its western side. Turtle Cove had a good landing beach, and inland, there was both a bridge and a ford across the Hutchinson River. The bridge connected with a road that led westward toward the retreating Americans, and the ford, known as the Wading Place, lay less than a mile north of the bridge.[4] The drawback of Pell's Point, as Howe would soon learn, was the presence of Colonel John Glover and his brigade.

A ship captain and merchant from Massachusetts, Glover was posted on the west side of the Hutchinson River across from the Split Rock, a picturesque frost-split glacial boulder that now lies in a far corner of Pelham Bay Park. Its crevasse was said to have sheltered the sole survivor of the massacre of Anne Hutchinson and her family in 1643, and the Split Rock was now to witness another episode of bloodshed.

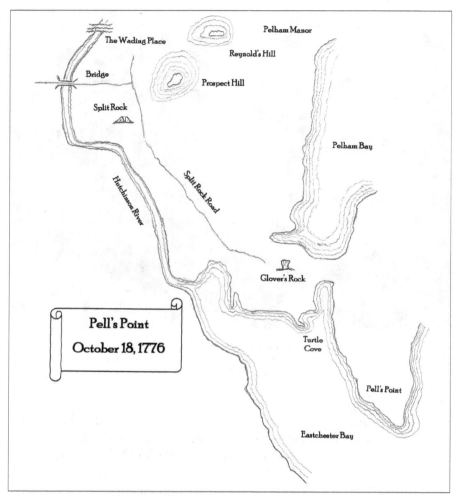

Map 2: Pell's Point, October 18, 1776. *Map by author.*

Years later, walkers on Split Rock Road would claim to hear the footsteps of a ghostly Native American woman rushing to warn Glover of the British landing.[5] Glover, though, had no need of spectral messengers that day to tell him the British were coming. He had sentinels posted along the coast, but before they could report, Glover, with his trusty captain's spyglass, had spotted the British masts from his high vantage point in present-day Mount Vernon. Before the last Hessian stepped ashore, Glover had his men in motion.

Leaving his three field guns on the west side of the Hutchinson River to cover his retreat, Glover opted to meet the enemy halfway. He posted his own Marblehead Regiment (Fourteenth Continental) as a reserve at the Split Rock and went ahead with his three remaining regiments to take up a defensive position on a rise of ground where the road wound through today's Split Rock Golf Course. With fewer than nine hundred men, Glover was badly outnumbered by Howe's four thousand, but as he later recalled, "I disposed of my little party to the best of my judgement." For once, Charles Lee had no advice to offer, as Glover's messenger was unable to locate the general, but Glover at least had a dependable brigade behind him, including the Marblehead Regiment.

One of the most unusual units in Washington's army, the Marblehead Regiment was composed of fishermen and mariners from Marblehead, Massachusetts, who had been thrown out of work by the British closure of the Grand Banks fishing grounds. Though seemingly strange material for an infantry regiment, they were nevertheless men accustomed to the discipline of teamwork and following orders—orders, moreover, given by a crusty sea captain colonel who did not deliberate over his decisions. The Marblehead Regiment had already proven its value to Washington; their maritime skills had enabled the midnight withdrawal of the army across the East River from Brooklyn, and they would do so again ten weeks later, when crossing the Delaware.

The Marbleheaders were unusual, too, in the high proportion—perhaps one-third—of men of color in their ranks, both Black and Native American. The maritime trade was one of the few industries in colonial America in which men of color could achieve something approaching equality. Regardless of ancestry, a seaman who pulled his weight could expect the same poor pay and ill treatment as anyone else on board, and having endured worse things than an afternoon firefight, the Marblehead men knew they could rely on each other.

It is worth noting that the Marblehead Regiment was far from unique in its enlistment of African Americans. Though most colonial militia laws excluded Black men from serving, several had taken part in the Battles of Concord and Bunker Hill. Anxious not to permit the enlistment of enslaved men and thereby open a path to emancipation, Congress, in January 1776, also enacted a moratorium on the enlistment of free Black men, but several states quietly ignored it in order to meet their recruitment quotas, and eventually, some five thousand African Americans would fight for the new United States. For the most part, they fought as part of integrated units,

A ghostly image of an African American soldier peers out from the polished black granite of a memorial in Middletown, Rhode Island. Men of color served on the Patriot side, notably in the Marblehead Regiment. *Photo by author.*

unlike those who adhered to the British, who were generally assigned to segregated rear echelon units.[6]

To deal with the oncoming British and Hessians, an outnumbered Glover decided on a New England–style defense, and in so doing, he would derail Howe's last opportunity to trap Washington. The area north of Pell's Point had largely been settled by Connecticut Yankees, and the Split Rock Road was lined by classic New England stone walls, perfect for the "skulking" kind of warfare that the British found so annoying. It was less than two miles from the beach at Turtle Cove to the bridge over the Hutchinson River, but for Howe, it would prove to be an agonizingly long two miles.

Complicating matters, the local militia had also been alerted and, unknown to Glover, had hurried down from Pelham Manor and taken up positions around a glacial boulder today known as Glover's Rock, just inland from the British landing beach.[7] Situated on a low hill overlooking

The militia confronted the British landing at Pell's Point near Glover's Rock, while Glover positioned his brigade nearly a mile to the north. *Photo by author.*

Though often disparaged, local militia could be dogged fighters when defending their own homes. *Library of Congress.*

Turtle Cove and Pelham Bay, Glover's Rock was a local landmark and a natural rallying point for the militia.

George Washington would often express his exasperation at ill-trained and panic-prone militia units, but when standing with their backs to their own dooryards, they could prove to be tenacious fighters. A Tory band with an armed sloop had been bedeviling the Long Island Sound coast all summer, so the men of Pelham were quick to turn out that October day, no doubt thinking it would be more of the same. It wasn't, but from their cover of shoreline shrubbery, they nevertheless opened fire on the assembling British and Hessians, causing them to pause and return fire.

About a mile away, Glover, perhaps puzzled by the sound of unexpected gunfire, finished getting his men into position. The militia soon broke off and fell back the way they came, passing through the wooded terrain east of Glover's position. Howe detailed a small force under George Cornwallis to pursue the militia while he turned his main force up the Split Rock Road.

There, they soon encountered Glover's men. Glover posted his three regiments behind stone walls, positioned so they could leapfrog each other. One regiment would open fire, but before the enemy could form up to storm their position, they would pull back behind a regiment manning another stone wall, and the process would be repeated. The first volleys revealed to Howe that he was up against not timorous militia but seasoned Continentals. Wildly overestimating the number of troops opposing him, Howe characteristically called a ninety-minute time-out, burning still more daylight while he deployed his soldiers and prepared for the main effort. He may have hoped the pause would prompt the Americans to rethink their situation and retreat. They didn't.

The wall-by-wall fighting along the Split Rock Road consumed most of what remained of the day. As evening approached, Glover had fallen back almost to the Split Rock when he received some worrisome news. By then, Cornwallis had birddogged the militia through the thick woods all the way to Pelham Manor, where the militia attempted a stand on Prospect Hill, overlooking the Hutchinson River. A sharp fight drove the militia off the hill, but instead of scattering, they regrouped on another hill to the north.

The unplanned intervention of the Pelham militia had led Cornwallis's task force around Glover's left flank, and the British were now in a position to seize the bridge over the Hutchinson and block Glover's access to the ford, thereby cutting off his line of retreat. Eyeing the still-feisty militiamen, though, Cornwallis made no move to descend from Prospect Hill. Before the British could change their minds, Glover wisely decided to call it a day

Top: The spectacular Split Rock was a rallying point for Glover's men. Local historian Toby Z. Liederman stands in the cleft. *Photo by Thomas X. Casey.*

Bottom: Reenactors of the Marblehead Regiment honor casualties of Pell's Point buried at the St. Paul's Church National Historic Site in Mount Vernon. *Photo by author.*

and brought his men across the bridge as the mid-October twilight settled in. The Battle of Pell's Point ended with a desultory artillery exchange between Glover's guns on the west bank of the Hutchinson River and the British fieldpieces on Prospect Hill. (A twelve-pound cannonball lobbed at the British was recently dug up in a Pelham backyard.)[8] As night fell, Glover led his men three miles to the northwest, edging closer to the main American army while still positioned to contest a westward advance by the British.

Having spent an entire day fighting over a two-mile stretch of country road of little strategic value, Howe again called a pause.[9] Setting up his headquarters in a manor house on the slope of Prospect Hill, he spent the following two days pondering his next move. It was now too late to intercept the retreating Americans, nor would he want to tangle again with those salty Yankees. Instead, on October 21, Howe marched his men up the coast to the port town of New Rochelle.

The old Huguenot haven of New Rochelle had a small harbor where Howe could rendezvous with the Royal Navy, which was bringing him supplies and reinforcements, with access to roads leading into central Westchester. Setting up his new headquarters at the ridgetop home of the Quaker James Pugsley, Howe was the guest of a family deeply divided by the war. Though three of James Pugsley's nephews were serving the Westchester Loyalist militia, his brother William was a captain in the rebel forces. James himself remained true to his Quaker pacifism, but the Loyalist associations of his family would nearly get his daughter Hannah murdered by Patriot vigilantes later in the war.

Asking no awkward questions of his host, Mr. Pugsley, Howe waited to see what opportunities the rebels might offer him. The rebels would soon show him that they were far from defeated. The smoke had scarcely cleared from the Pell's Point fight when the Marbleheaders struck again. The men of Marblehead were as well known for smuggling as they were for fishing, and these stealthy skills came in handy when, on the night of October 20–21, they penetrated the town of Eastchester to recover a cache of supplies that the British had failed to locate and secure. Almost under the noses of a nearby British encampment, they loaded up and made off with some two hundred precious barrels of pork and flour, all without a shot being fired.

More serious trouble would come two nights later with a nocturnal clash between two of the more colorful units in the war.

Chapter 4

SKIRMISH AT HEATHCOTE HILL

As Howe settled into New Rochelle, he rendezvoused with the Queen's Rangers, the same Loyalist unit that had spent the summer scouring the shores of Long Island Sound with their armed sloop, raiding and stirring up mayhem that did little for the cause of King George. An illustrious history and a celebrity commander had secured them many recruits, and by October 1776, the Queen's Rangers had grown to a strength of nearly four hundred.

Their commander, Colonel Robert Rogers, was a legend in his own time, a hero of the French and Indian War. It was Rogers who, in 1755, had organized the American Rangers and led them in such exploits as the Battle on Snowshoes and an epic long-distance raid on the hitherto untouchable French-allied Abenaki Indians. At first skeptical of the value of such an independent band of frontier scouts who followed their own rules and devised their own tactics for forest fighting, British generals came to depend on them for security and intelligence, and Rogers was a renowned figure with the rank of major by the time the unit was disbanded in 1761, shortly before the close of the war in 1763.

The years since then, though, had not been kind to this onetime hero, and when the Massachusetts-born Rogers offered his services to the Americans, a suspicious George Washington had him arrested as a spy. Slipping out of captivity, Rogers promptly went over to the British side, forming a Loyalist Queen's Rangers that sought to replicate the renown of his old unit.

Awaiting the British invasion, the Queen's Rangers had been something of a unit without a mission, so Rogers got hold of a small armed sloop and used it to raid Patriot farmsteads along the Long Island and Westchester shores. Moonlighting as a counterintelligence operative, Rogers himself also claimed credit for "outing" the American spy Nathan Hale shortly after he landed on Long Island, seeing through Hale's thin disguise as an itinerant schoolmaster and tricking him into revealing his mission over a convivial beer at a Long Island tavern.

Despite his fame in legend and tavern tales, the sad truth was that, in 1776, neither Rogers nor his rangers were what they used to be. Drink and disappointment had taken much of the fire out of Rogers, and instead of the hand-picked frontiersmen he led in the old days, the new rangers were mostly sons of farmers, eager for adventure and the pizzazz of wearing the distinctive green rangers cap. Training, discipline and woodcraft skills were also lax. Rogers's 1757 "Rules for Ranging" are to this day printed in the U.S. Army Rangers handbook, but in 1776, Rogers was no longer living up to them.

Commanding the Queen's Rangers in 1776, Robert Rogers was no longer living up to his French and Indian War legend and would suffer embarrassment at Heathcote Hill. *Library of Congress.*

Not entirely sure what to make of this scruffy band, Howe posted them at Heathcote Hill, overlooking the harbor of Mamaroneck, north of New Rochelle. There, they would be in a position to keep an eye on the Americans gathering at White Plains, blunt any aggressive probes from that direction and perhaps launch a raid or two that would discombobulate the rebels. The rebels, though, would hit Rogers first.

Washington's forces had no sooner begun to arrive at White Plains on October 22 than Colonel John Haslet's Delaware Regiment was detailed to make a surprise nighttime attack on the Queen's Rangers, who were temptingly encamped a mere five miles away. Reports by spies and deserters had produced a reasonably clear picture of the disposition of the British forces, so Haslet was able to plan a secure route by which he could strike at Rogers.

The selection of Haslet and his Delaware Regiment was no casual choice. A well-funded state militia unit, the Delaware Regiment was one of the few units in the newborn American army that reported for duty well drilled, fully armed and consistently uniformed. Their blue-coated uniforms indeed made them a standout in the motley-clad American encampment. Dubbed the "Delaware Blues" or, more humorously, the "Blue Hen's Chickens,"[10] the Delaware men came to White Plains with a well-established reputation for valor. At the Battle of Brooklyn on August 27, they supported a desperate counterattack by the Maryland Regiment that enabled a significant portion of the defeated Americans to escape a British encirclement, thereby preventing a defeat from turning into a catastrophe that could have effectively ended the American resistance. (A monument to the Delaware Regiment stands today near the battle site in Brooklyn's Green-Wood Cemetery.) Steadfast and dependable, the Delaware Regiment was a unit Washington could turn to in difficult situations.

The Delaware Regiment's commander, Ulster-born John Haslet, brought an unusual background to his military service. He was an ordained Presbyterian minister in his native Ireland but switched his profession to physician when he emigrated to America. Despite his patchwork career—preacher, doctor and now colonel—Haslet nevertheless had a reputation as a reliable officer who knew how to lead men in battle.[11]

Haslet's approach to the rangers' camp called for a bit of finesse, as they would pass within two miles of another British encampment (around what today is the first tee of the Bonnie Brae Golf Course). Luckily, Rogers had violated his own safety rules by posting only one sentry to guard the approach route. This lone ranger was quickly dispatched, but Haslet's luck ran out when his men found themselves stepping on the forms of some sixty rangers snoozing in a detached bivouac.

The rudely awakened men raised the alarm, and the Delaware Blues found themselves in a firefight as they approached the main ranger camp atop Heathcote Hill. The advantage of surprise lost, Haslet broke off the action before the gunfire could rouse any nearby redcoats. Still, he took thirty-six prisoners, and his men quickly scavenged the abandoned bivouac, scooping up sixty stands of arms and, perhaps most valuable of all, as many woolen blankets. All in all, it had been a good night's work for the Blue Hen's Chickens.

The results of the Skirmish of Heathcote's Hill (as a modern historical marker puts it) may have been less than the Americans hoped for, but it showed yet again that they were far from a cowed force of beaten men. It

The surprise attack by the Delaware Blues on the Queen's Rangers at Heathcote Hill demonstrated American aggressiveness days before the Battle of White Plains. *Photo by author.*

also raised troubling questions among the British command about the value of the vaunted Queen's Rangers, who, after all, were supposed to surprise the enemy, not the other way around. Howe would leave the Queen's Rangers in the rear echelons for the remainder of the campaign, and Heathcote Hill would be the beginning of the downfall of the legendary Robert Rogers, who would finally be sacked from command early in the new year.

Two skirmishes on the following day, October 23, further demonstrated that the Americans were not to be trifled with. Captain Johann Ewald took two companies of Hessian jägers across the Bronx River to probe the American rear guard in the vicinity of Mile Square, only to run afoul of Colonel Edward Hand's Pennsylvania riflemen. Having stymied the British and Hessians at Throggs Neck, the riflemen were eager to take on the jägers. It was a rare example of rifle versus rifle combat in the Revolutionary War, and for the newly arrived Hessian jägers, it was their first contact with the American rebels.

The Hessian jägers (German for "hunters") whom Ewald commanded were a specialized corps recruited from professional huntsmen and gamekeepers on German aristocratic estates. Uniformed in green, the jägers were accustomed to the forest, and they were skilled marksmen (after all, a charging boar seldom allowed for a second shot). Serving as scouts and skirmishers, the jägers carried short-barreled rifles that, while they didn't have quite the range of the long Pennsylvania rifles, were handier to deploy in thick woods.

What began as a chance skirmish soon spun out of control into a serious engagement as nearby American troops joined in the fray. Ewald himself noted in his diary that he had set out that morning wishing for "nothing more than to get to know the enemy."[12] The day would prove to be a chastening experience for him. The one-eyed Ewald would serve right up to the surrender at Yorktown in 1781 and become a recognized authority on small unit tactics, but he would ever after respect the fighting prowess of the American rebels.

In the sharp action at Mile Square, the jägers lost six men; eleven were wounded (four mortally) and two were missing. They might have found themselves surrounded and trapped on the far side of the Bronx River had not a rescue force of the Scottish Forty-Second Highland Regiment (known as the Black Watch) intervened to bail them out.

Serving in the multinational force that Howe commanded, the Black Watch was a singularly picturesque unit. They were one of two Gaelic-speaking Scottish Highland regiments in the British force. Impressed with the fighting fury the Highlanders had displayed in Scottish uprisings, the British government organized the Forty-Second in 1739, at first to police the restive Highlands and later for use as shock troops in their expanding empire. Clad in the dark blue-green tartan kilts that gave them their nickname and wielding basket-hilted broadswords in addition to dirks, pistols and muskets, the men of the Forty-Second had proved their worth in the Battle of Brooklyn and would serve with distinction throughout the war.

Meanwhile, for the Hessians, even such a mundane mission as doing the laundry could prove hazardous in the presence of aggressive Americans. While the Pennsylvania men slugged it out with the jägers and Highlanders, on another part of the Bronx River, an American patrol, backed by a detachment of Glover's Marbleheaders, attacked a Hessian outpost whose men had come to the riverbank to launder their officers' shirts. They killed ten Hessians, took three prisoners and claimed a Hessian officer's horse along with three tubs full of freshly washed shirts, itself a worthy prize in an increasingly ragtag army.

The Bronx River was still relatively easy to ford on October 23, but this situation was not going to last.

Chapter 5

APPROACH TO WHITE PLAINS

Reinforced by the arrival of additional British and Hessians, on October 25, Howe at last got the main body of his army in motion and marched out of New Rochelle, advancing by way of present-day Weaver Street and Mamaroneck Road in the direction of White Plains. Slowed down by muddy roads and uncertainty about the terrain, they advanced only as far as Scarsdale, a mere three miles from White Plains. Named after an aristocratic manor in old England, Scarsdale was an agreeable place for the British to enjoy a bit of repose as the soldiers pitched their camps in the fields along the Post Road.

The window of opportunity for victory, though, was rapidly slipping away as Washington consolidated his position at White Plains. A more vigorous march might have surprised the rebels on October 25 with their fortifications not yet complete. Howe's move had, curiously, gone undetected by American spies and scouts, and Washington only learned of it when the British arrived in Scarsdale. Fearing an imminent attack, the Americans redoubled their fortification work. The British, though, were not coming that day, nor the day after. Nor the day after that.

Howe instead paused at Scarsdale for another two days. He was concerned that too rapid an advance to White Plains would leave his rear open to possible assault from General Lee's division that was still making its way up the opposite side of the Bronx River. Howe may have detested Charles Lee as a turncoat, but he respected his military professionalism and was wary of a sudden aggressive move on Lee's part. Commanding Washington's rear

For his headquarters, General Howe took over the Griffin House, which still stands today as a private residence on Fenimore Road in Scarsdale. *Photo by author.*

guard, Lee, ironically, feared the same thing from Howe, and he detoured his men westward, away from the river, to eventually make their way into White Plains via the Dobbs Ferry Road. British scouts could plainly see Lee's men marching up from Mile Square and itched to attack them, but the orders never came. And the river was rising.

Howe wasn't sure what Washington was up to, but it looked as if, instead of continuing his northward retreat, he was preparing to make a stand at White Plains. If Howe could draw Washington onto open ground, he would have one more chance to destroy the rebel army, and a locale with a name like White Plains seemed a good place to do it.

The county seat of Westchester since 1757 and briefly the capital of New York when the Provincial Congress met there in July 1776, the small town of White Plains was the meeting place of several key roads. The York Road (present-day Post Road) ran north from the lower end of the county and served as the town's main street before continuing farther north. Roads coming from the east from New Rochelle, Mamaroneck, Bedford and Connecticut all met at White Plains, and a bridge across the Bronx River connected them to roads leading west to Dobbs Ferry and Tarrytown on the Hudson River and to Robbins Mills (later Kensico) to the north.

White Plains was described as a "beautiful little town situate on a commodious plain"[13] by Pennsylvania rifleman James McMichael, and the town's buildings were for the most part located along the York Road. The White Plains, or "the Plains," as the landscape was commonly known, stretched westward between the town and the Bronx River, where local farmers tilled fields of corn and wheat. The peaceful bucolic scenery, though, belied a countryside already riven by the conflict.

A tale of two taverns illustrates the political divisions of White Plains in 1776. Isaac Oakley's tavern on today's South Broadway was the gathering place for rebellious-minded locals, and Isaac himself would serve as a guide for the rebel army. Across the street, next to the courthouse, Captain Abraham Hatfield's tavern was the Loyalist hangout. In April 1775, 312 Loyalists gathered at Hatfield's to sign a statement affirming their determination "at the hazard of our lives and properties, to support the King and Constitution."

The Loyalist turnout was not surprising. The lands west of the river were part of Philipse Manor, stretching from Spuyten Duyvil to the Croton River, all owned by the staunch Tory Frederick Philipse III. Some farmers in White Plains leased land in Philipse Manor, where Frederick, as absolute landlord, could compel obedience from his tenants on pain of immediate eviction.

Confident of a British victory, a month after the battle, on November 28, Philipse drew up a "Declaration of *De*pendence" and demanded that his tenants put their names to it. For a tenant farmer with no right of tenure, it was a simple matter of sign it—or else.

The conflict divided not only the town but also many families within it. Old Captain Hatfield died in November 1775, a few months after producing his own Loyalist statement, but two of his nephews, Joshua and Daniel, would fight on the American side in the coming battle less than a year later. Several other members of the extended Hatfield clan would persist as Loyalists, and as a result, they would be exiled to Nova Scotia at the end of the war.[14]

For a general seeking a battlefield who was unfamiliar with the place, the name White Plains could be misleading. If Howe thought he would encounter a flat ground suitable for the tabletop maneuvers of European warfare, he was to be disappointed. Reconnaissance showed that the White Plains landscape was interspersed with low rolling hills and was divided by Golden Pine Brook (today's Davis Brook), which flowed northward toward the Bronx River through patches of boggy ground. (Inspired by the morning mists rising from the Bronx River, the Native Americans named the area Quarropas, or "white marsh," a more accurate description.) This was far from a broad field for maneuver—not that Washington was going to offer the sort of chessboard battle he knew by now the British excelled at.

Howe's dallying at New Rochelle and Scarsdale had by now gifted Washington with more than five precious days in which to deploy his troops, prepare his defenses and, above all, secure those invaluable supplies and get them moving on the road to Fishkill.

For both the American and British armies, there were never enough wagons, along with their ornery drivers, who had to be persuaded or compelled to move their heavily laden wagons through an active war zone. The pace of the ox-drawn wagon train, perhaps two miles an hour at best, dictated Washington's defensive strategy; the road to Fishkill led to a bottleneck where Pine's Bridge offered the only way to cross the fast-flowing Croton River. Not for nothing had the native Wappingers named the river the Kitchawan, or "swift water"; fording it could be hazardous even in dry weather and all but impossible in wetter seasons.[15]

Pine's Bridge was built by and named for two carpenter brothers, Peter and John Pyne, both committed Patriots who took up the bridge's planks every night to frustrate Tory raiders—or anyone trying to sneak across without paying them a toll. There were at least two fords and a ferry downstream to the west, but none of them were suitable for crossing a fully loaded wagon

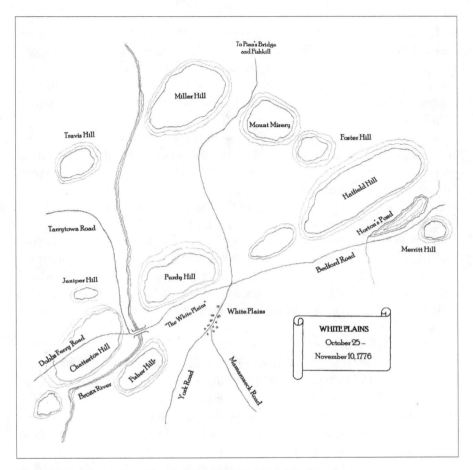

To Pine's Bridge
and Fishkill

Miller Hill

Mount Misery

Travis Hill

Foster Hill

Hatfield Hill

Tarrytown Road

Horton's Pond

Merritt Hill

Juniper Hill

Purdy Hill

Bedford Road

"The White Plains"

White Plains

WHITE PLAINS
October 25 –
November 10, 1776

Dobbs Ferry Road

Chatterton Hill

Fisher Hill

Bronx River

York Road

Mamaroneck Road

Map 3: White Plains, October 25–November 10, 1776. *Map by author.*

train, so it was vital that Washington deny the road to Pine's Bridge to the British until the wagons had made it safely across the Croton.

The Pine's Bridge crossing would have been vulnerable to being cut off by a sweeping cavalry raid—had not the British force been deficient in cavalry and uncertain as to the terrain north of White Plains. Taking no chances, though, Washington detailed three Maryland regiments to stand guard over the high ground south of the Croton River, in case the British tried any creative maneuvers.

Once on the north side of the Croton, the wagons would at least be in friendlier territory. Like the western half of southern Westchester County, most of present-day Putnam County was owned by the Loyalist Philipse family and was variously known as the Upper Philipse Patent, the Highland Patent or the more grandiose Philipi. About ten years before, the area had seen a brief rent war ignited by tenants protesting the exactions of the Philipses, and though the uprising was quashed, the resentments had long festered, leaving most of the area's inhabitants with little love for Frederick Philipse or the king he supported.[16]

The wagon train's destination was the new Continental supply base at Fishkill. Tucked in among defensible hills about five miles inland from present-day Beacon, on the upper reach of the Hudson north of West Point, Fishkill was, for the time being, reasonably secure from surprise British raids, and it was connected by road both to Connecticut and to the river ports of Poughkeepsie and Fishkill Landing (Beacon).[17]

Once White Plains was emptied of the army's provisions, Washington had no need to contest control of the town but had only to maintain his position in the hills for the next few days. Dug in on what some would term Howe's Hell Hills, the Americans were ready to fight; morale rose with each shovelful, as the rising breastworks raised the specter of another Bunker Hill.[18]

Howe's Hell Hills were aptly named. North of the plains, the rolling terrain abruptly ended in a chain of hills that marked the southern end of the rugged Hudson Highlands, offering Howe a forbidding prospect to assault, and the terrain only grew worse as one moved farther north. For Washington, one advantage at least of commanding an army of farmers was that these men, tilling the stony glacial soil of New York and New England, were accustomed to the work of digging ditches and moving rocks. Commanded to fortify their assigned positions, they didn't need to be told twice.

Arriving with the army's rear guard, General Charles Lee was unimpressed with the layout of the American positions and, as usual, was quick to offer Washington his advice. Taking Washington on a reconnoitering ride to the hills of North Castle, a couple of miles above the White Plains entrenchments, Lee pointed out the stony heights of Miller Hill and Mount Misery. "Yonder," he told his commander, "is the ground we ought to occupy."[19] Washington could only agree, but with the British advance imminent, it was a bit late to change things. Instead, he quietly ordered reserve units to begin fortifying these positions as a second line of defense. Washington also joined Lee in establishing his headquarters at the home of Ann Fisher Miller.

Bearing the names of two of the area's longest-settled families, Ann (short for Annatjie) now found herself hostess to the American high

Left: Washington's second-in-command, Charles Lee, urged Washington to establish a line of defense north of White Plains in the hills of North Castle. *Library of Congress*

Below: As the British approached White Plains, Washington transferred his headquarters to the Miller House, sharing it with Charles Lee. *Photo by author.*

command. The war, though, had arrived on her doorstep long before. Her husband, Elijah, had marched off in the spring with the Third Regiment of the Westchester County Militia to defend Manhattan, only to be carried home to die on August 21 of wounds received in an unrecorded affray at Hell Gate on the East River.[20] Two of her sons, John and Elijah Jr., were still serving in their dad's unit, somewhere in the hills above White Plains. To the end of her long life, Ann would be proud of her service in the Revolution, but what she made of such mismatched houseguests as the gentlemanly George Washington and the rough-mannered Charles Lee seems to have been left unrecorded.

Tucked beneath the western slope of Miller Hill, Ann's house was a more secure location than the exposed home of Washington's earlier hostess, Abagail Smith Purdy, at the northern edge of the White Plains. Abagail's home was literally on the front line, facing the expected British attack along the forward entrenchments dug by the local militia just before Washington's arrival. Like many of her neighbors, Abagail was of Connecticut Yankee stock; married into the prominent and prolific Purdy family, she herself was descended from the Puritan worthy the Reverend Thomas Hooker, founder of Hartford, Connecticut.

With her house in the line of fire and her husband, Jacob, serving in the Second Regiment of the Westchester County Militia, Abagail sought shelter for her family among her many relatives in the area. But not all would be welcoming. The Purdys, like so many other Westchester families, were a family divided by the war. Jacob's youngest brother, Gabriel, was with Howe's army as a Loyalist volunteer; outspoken in his support of King George, Gabriel was one of twenty-six Purdys who had signed the Loyalist declaration at Hatfield's tavern the year before. Abagail instead found refuge a few miles to the north at her sister's house at Robbins Mills.

Rising behind Abagail's house, Purdy Hill, alongside the rain-swollen Bronx River, was the western anchor of Washington's original line of defense. The Americans were dug in near the crest of the hill amid Abigail's apple trees, an agreeable enough place with the sweet autumn scent of wind-fallen fruit. From Purdy Hill, the main line of entrenchments ran east over a slight dip in the terrain, crossed the York Road and continued on to the heights of Hatfield Hill. Horton's Millpond, formed by damming the headwaters of the Mamaroneck River, formed a protective barrier to the south of Hatfield Hill, and across the eastern end of the millpond, Merritt Hill lay at the far end of the American line, athwart the road to Connecticut.

Headquartered in the hillside farmhouse of Gilbert Hatfield, General William Heath was the division commander tasked with holding the American left flank. The thirty-nine-year-old Heath in many ways exemplified the American ideal of the farmer-citizen-soldier. Born on a Massachusetts farm that his family had owned since 1636, Heath, as a brigadier general of the militia, took command of the American forces in the later stages of the Battle of Lexington and Concord.

Never an excitable sort, Heath was sanguine about his situation. Hatfield Hill hardly needed fortifying, and the entrenchments on Merritt Hill would

Michael Grillo, portraying George Washington, greets a fellow reenactor at the Purdy House, which briefly served as Washington's headquarters in October 1776. *Photo by author.*

hopefully discourage any British flanking maneuvers. A steep upthrust of hard bedrock, Hatfield Hill was possibly the strongest position occupied by the Americans at this time. Successive advances and meltbacks of ice age glaciers had left the slopes strewn with boulders and ravines, a veritable devil's rock garden that provided innumerable places where defending forces could shelter and fire down at struggling attackers. Steep, stony and heavily wooded, Hatfield Hill also had an eerie look about it. The place was said to be haunted by the apparition of a white deer, but if the spooky white deer made an appearance that week, the hungry soldiers no doubt would have shot it.[21]

While William Heath commanded the American left wing, another William oversaw the right. The curiously titled Lord Stirling commanded a brigade covering Washington's flank on Purdy and Chatterton Hills. His adopted title may seem at odds with the assumption that aristocrats naturally belonged on the British side, and history has tended to dismiss Lord Stirling as an eccentric poseur. His birth name was William Alexander, but he was nevertheless a lord. An ironmaster from New Jersey whose lands were blessed by veins of incredibly rich iron ore, Alexander spent years in Britain pursuing a lawsuit to establish his claim as the rightful heir of the Scottish earldom of Stirling, which, among other things, would have landed him a seat in the House of Lords.[22] The courts eventually found in his favor, but the House of Lords declined to bestow the title. A disappointed Alexander returned home to his iron furnaces but adopted the title of Lord Stirling anyway, and the ever-punctilious Washington invariably addressed him as such.

Stirling's iron mines and furnaces were an invaluable resource for the new American nation then and for many years after. Iron from the Hudson Highlands, the country's premier source of iron and copper, would later be used to forge the great chain stretched across the Hudson River at West Point to deny navigation to British warships. As America's first heavy industry, the iron business was no place for gentle souls, and his experience as an ironmaster gave Stirling invaluable managerial skills, both in running a complex business and directing a hard-knuckled workforce. A committed Patriot despite his aristocratic title, Stirling's stubborn defense of the American extreme right flank at the Battle of Brooklyn won Washington's respect, even though Stirling himself was captured in the process. Stirling had been exchanged just three weeks before and was back in his former command, and Washington now depended on him to show the same tenacity and dedication at White Plains.

Lord Stirling, in turn, depended on his namesake and fellow Scotsman General Alexander McDougall to hold Chatterton Hill—or at least make the British pay dearly for it. Born on the Hebridean Isle of Islay (where he is today commemorated by a monument), McDougall had a colorful career as a merchant and privateer captain, as well as a leader of the Sons of Liberty

Left: Rightful heir to a Scottish earldom, Lord Stirling (William Alexander) commanded the western extremity of Washington's lines, including Chatterton Hill. *New York Public Library.*

Right: The redoubtable Israel Putnam commanded Washington's right wing on Purdy Hill. *Library of Congress.*

in New York City (Greenwich Village's iconic McDougall Street is named for him). Like Stirling, McDougall knew a few things about handling rowdy sailors, having often enough been one of them himself.[23]

Commanding the entrenchments on Purdy Hill was General Israel Putnam, or Old Put, as he was generally known. Like McDougall and Lord Sterling, Old Put had a colorful background. Twenty years before, in the French and Indian War, the grandfatherly general had been one of the toughest of the legendary Rogers's Rangers, rising to the rank of major; his exploits nearly matched those of Robert Rogers himself. He also had a curious connection with the enemy commander at White Plains; on July 6, 1758, he had been with William Howe's older brother George Augustus, Lord Howe, moments before he was fatally shot near Fort Ticonderoga and had urged him not to endanger himself by going forward. The unfortunate George Augustus was still revered by many Americans as a hero, even while his younger brother William was now reviled as a villain.

Back home, Old Put was renowned as the sort of fellow who would crawl headfirst into a rocky den to shoot what was reputed to be the last wolf in Connecticut, a tale no doubt recounted around Continental campfires. Like the legendary Roman Cincinnatus, Putnam was said to have abandoned his plow midfield to join the fighting outside Boston, and he never looked back. He enjoyed a good rapport with his soldiers, who admired him for his courage and common touch, and Washington regarded him as one of his most dependable officers.

Putnam, Stirling and McDougall would command the critical part of the Battle of White Plains as Howe prepared to assault Chatterton Hill.

Chapter 6

ASSAULT ON CHATTERTON HILL

S outh of Purdy Hill on the western bank of the Bronx River, Chatterton Hill had been something of an afterthought to the American plans for defense. Washington at first had given it little regard, but Charles Lee recommended occupying it. A force atop Chatterton Hill would further secure the American right flank on Purdy Hill, as well as hold the Chatterton Bridge over the Bronx River while posing a threat to Howe's left flank should he deploy on the White Plains. It would also serve as a fallback position for General Joseph Spencer's brigade, which was posted on the Fenimore Road south of White Plains to give early warning of the British advance from Scarsdale. Now an upscale neighborhood known as Battle Hill, Chatterton Hill would prove crucial to the outcome of the Battle of White Plains.

Like its neighbors Purdy Hill and Hatfield Hill, Chatterton Hill was another steep up thrust of bedrock, a legacy of long-ago continental collisions. It rose 180 feet above the Bronx River, its long axis paralleling the river and presenting a steep, broad side facing the White Plains. It was a strong defensive position, but its geology in some ways worked against its defenders; the middle of the hilltop had enough soil for cornfields, but the hill's rocky spine ran along its eastern edge, making it impossible to dig trenches there, where they were most needed. Instead, the 1,600 men assigned to defend the hill scavenged farmer Michael Chatterton's recently harvested cornfields, tearing up the empty stalks and piling them into something resembling breastworks. These cornstalk fortifications wouldn't stop much of anything, but they gave the troops a degree of psychological comfort and, from a distance, looked formidable enough.

Chatterton Hill as viewed from White Plains. The Dobbs Ferry Road can be seen curving up the middle. *Benson Lossing,* Pictorial Field Book of the Revolution.

CHATTERTON'S HILL, FROM THE RAIL-WAY STATION.

It wouldn't be long before the cornstalks were put to the test. Early on the morning of October 28, Howe roused his army and set out on the short march to the White Plains, following the Mamaroneck Road north from Scarsdale. At the Secor Fork, named for the farming family of that name, the Fenimore Road branched off to the west, connecting the Mamaroneck Road with the York Road. Dividing his army into two columns to speed the march, Howe sent de Heister's Hessians down the Fenimore Road to the York Road, while the right-hand column under Henry Clinton would continue on the Mamaroneck Road, with the two eventually meeting at the White Plains.[24]

Along the Fenimore Road, de Heister's advance guard ran into Spencer's division, which was hunkered down behind stone walls, ready to contest the Hessian advance. A French and Indian War veteran, Major General Joseph Spencer was considered one of the best officers in the American army. This was perhaps more than could be said of the men he commanded that day, who were mostly untried Connecticut militiamen. Spencer's mission, though, was not to attempt a heroic stand but only to "give the enemy as much annoyance as possible on their approach" and provide a report on their movements.[25] In modern-day military parlance, Spencer's mission was to serve as a speed bump.

Among the troops engaged in Spencer's spoiling action was a young Connecticut militiaman named Joseph Plumb Martin. A month shy of his sixteenth birthday, Martin was already a veteran of the battle for Manhattan. He had been out foraging for turnip tops when the British began their advance from Scarsdale. With no time to cook his turnip tops, he hastily packed up his utensils and pocket Bible and took up a position behind a stone wall to face the Hessian onslaught.[26]

The fields along Fenimore Road were crisscrossed by high stone walls, ideal for an American defense. From behind their stone walls, the Connecticut men opened fire and gave the Hessians a rough handling at first, inflicting significant casualties and prompting them to fall back and regroup. Renewing

The opening shots of the Battle of White Plains were fired in Scarsdale, where Colonel Joseph Spencer used stone walls along the Fenimore Road to contest the Hessian advance. *Photo by author.*

the attack, the Hessians were joined by some mounted dragoons, the sight of whom was enough to spark panic in the militiamen, who bolted for the Bronx River, some throwing down their muskets in their pell-mell flight.

The Connecticut men had good reason for their hurried departure. Though few in number, the Hessian dragoons were indeed a sight to be feared. Hailing from Hesse-Cassel, they were essentially mounted infantry. Armed with heavy long swords along with muskets and pistols, they were trained to fight either on foot or on horseback as the occasion required. When running down fleeing infantry, *dragoon* was a byword for ruthlessness, but the pursuit that day was hampered by those troublesome stone walls. Unable to vault the high walls, the dragoons were forced to lose time and momentum by riding around them.

Hotly pursued by the Hessians, Spencer kept his men together as best he could and retreated through the area known today as Greenacres toward a ford in the Bronx River that would bring them to the safety of Chatterton Hill. The Bronx River today bends slightly west at the southeastern corner of Chatterton Hill before resuming a more southerly course. In 1776, that oxbow may have curved somewhat farther to the west, lapping the southern face of Chatterton Hill. Such river bends often accumulate sandbanks along their inner curves, creating fords.[27]

This did not necessarily mean an easy crossing. The Bronx River today is called by environmentalists a flashy river. It flows down through a relatively narrow rocky valley, and even moderate rainfall causes the river to rapidly rise. In 1776, before the Kensico Dam cut off its headwaters, the river likely carried a greater volume of water to begin with. Though not at flood stage, the Bronx River was running high that day after the recent rainy weather, and even at the ford, the water was chest high. With the enemy hard on their heels, though, Spencer's men went across without a second thought, while the Hessians hesitated to wade in.

Colonel Johann Rall, commanding a Hessian brigade, nevertheless ordered his men across while the others stood and stared at the swirling waters. Emerging from the ford, Rall ordered his sopping soldiers to pursue Spencer up the hillside. Spencer's men, though, had kept their powder dry; halfway up the hill, they turned and delivered a discouraging volley. Rall,

Resplendent in their tall brass miter hats, the Hessians were a fearsome sight on the battlefield. *Photo by author.*

reconsidering the wisdom of pursuing an unsupported assault, pulled his men back to occupy a low rise south of Chatterton Hill near the village of Hart's Corners (today's Hartsdale). Leaving his men to wring out their uniforms, Rall awaited orders while keeping a chary eye on the Americans.[28]

With most of his army arriving at the White Plains, Howe, traveling behind his left-hand column, was now aware of the threat posed by Chatterton Hill. If Howe had been planning an immediate frontal assault on the rebel lines, the troops atop Chatterton Hill forced him to reconsider. Military wisdom, then as now, frowned on making a frontal assault while ignoring an enemy force that could threaten your flank and rear. Fighting in linear formations, men couldn't fire in two directions at once, and even a small attack coming at their side or rear could throw a battle formation into disarray. By now wary of American aggressiveness, Howe had little choice; before launching any attack on Washington's main line, he would first have to clear Chatterton Hill.

An alternative strategy would have been to ignore Chatterton Hill and instead make an end run around the eastern extreme of the American line, but this idea was quashed when a cavalry reconnaissance revealed that the Americans had dug in on Merritt Hill. A single cannon shot was enough to convince the British that the Americans there meant business, and observation of the terrain revealed that even if an attack could force its way past Merritt Hill and work its way around the east end of Horton's Mill Pond, it would only run up against Heath's main force, dug in on Hatfield Hill. Chatterton Hill, then, would be Howe's choice for the opening attack.

Seizing Chatterton Bridge at the north end of the hill carried the risk of getting a force caught between the fire from Chatterton Hill and that from Washington's forward entrenchments, as well as cannon fire from Purdy Hill. Howe instead decided on an assault across the ford at the south end of the hill, away from the forward entrenchments and out of range of Purdy Hill.

Ordering the assault, Howe was taken aback by what he took to be the refusal of the Hessian commander de Heister to send his soldiers into the high waters of the ford. By now, Howe was growing increasingly annoyed with this obstreperous Hessian, who had dragged his feet before the Battle of Brooklyn and was now seemingly doing so again. By the conventional rules of seniority, the sixty-year-old de Heister was second-in-command of the combined British-Hessian army, but Howe had taken the precaution of drawing up a "dormant commission" that would place Henry Clinton in command should anything happen to him. It was to Clinton that Howe now turned, and he rode off to find him.

It was all perhaps a misunderstanding in this linguistically challenged partnership. Hoping to avoid using the ford, de Heister's men were just then trying to improvise a bridge across the Bronx River out of felled trees and fence rails.[29] Located about halfway between the ford and the Chatterton Bridge, this may not have been the best place to launch an assault on Chatterton Hill. In any event, the bridge project didn't work out, and when Howe returned with Clinton, he found de Heister's men entering the ford anyway. It was now past noon on a short October day.

Howe directed the brigade commanded by General Alexander Leslie to join in the attack. The personal frictions of the campaign were piling up; Howe was annoyed with Leslie, too, for allowing the chance skirmish at Harlem Heights a few weeks before to blossom into a nearly full-blown battle that cost 140 British dead and wounded for no purpose. Leslie, commanding the rear of the army, was nevertheless the man on the spot, and at least he spoke English.

Atop Chatterton Hill, Alexander McDougall took command of the American units and sorted them into a defensive formation. Joseph Spencer's arriving troops were placed in the fields along the southwest slope to dry out in the sunshine. Smallwood's Maryland Regiment was placed on the right center, supported by the Sixth Regiment of Dutchess County Militia. Colonel John Brooks's Massachusetts Militia was placed alongside the Delaware Blues just south of the hill's crest; like Delaware's John Haslet, Brooks had been trained as a physician, swapping his scalpel for a sword at the outbreak of the Revolution. The First and Third New York, along with the Connecticut Militia, held the center of the line, facing east toward the White Plains, with Webb's Nineteenth Continental at the extreme left, overlooking the Dobbs Ferry Road. Though appearing to be a mixed bag of units, these dispositions would prove crucial to the outcome of the fight; by accident or design, the best veteran regiments on the hill were positioned to receive the brunt of the British assault.[30]

For the British, the key to assaulting Chatterton Hill lay just across the river at Fisher Hill, then known as Wolf Pit Hill for the traps dug there in the valley's wilder days.[31] The hill's elevation was only slightly less than Chatterton's, offering a platform from which artillery could bombard the Americans. Fisher's eastern slope fronted on the York Road, and a farm lane ran up its side, making it easy to haul artillery up to good firing positions. The top of the hill, east of present-day Rochambeau High School, was about seven hundred yards from the American positions, a good range for both cannons and howitzers.

The nimble three-pounder was a battlefield mainstay. Two of these guns were dispatched to Chatterton Hill. *Photo by author.*

Cannons, though, were a bit of a problem. Howe deployed eight British fieldpieces to Fisher Hill, but for some strange reason, the guns had become separated from their crews. Handling a cannon required a well-drilled team, so Howe borrowed naval gun crews from his brother Richard to get the job done. Accustomed to naval warfare, where nearly all shots were fired point-blank, the sailors weren't versed in the finer points of elevation and ballistics needed to effectively target the men atop Chatterton Hill. Luckily, de Heister had brought his own guns along, and the fifteen Hessian pieces included howitzers—with experienced crews to man them.

Long-barreled cannons were the workhorses of the eighteenth-century battlefield, distinguished according to the weight of the cannonballs they fired, ranging from the nimble three-pounder "grasshopper" to the bruising twenty-four-pounder and the fort-busting thirty-six-pounder. For close-up work, cannons could also fire grapeshot, a cluster of small iron balls that made the cannon into a shotgun the size of a drainpipe. Mounted on a wheeled gun carriage, the cannon's tremendous recoil meant that it couldn't be elevated more than a few degrees without damaging its carriage. Cannons could shoot an iron ball up to two thousand yards, though their most effective range was one thousand yards or less.

Such iron balls, or solid shot, could do horrible damage; one veteran on Chatterton Hill watched aghast as a single cannonball smashed a man's head open, took another man's arm off, disemboweled a third man and finally fractured a fourth man's hip. It was said that you only saw a cannonball in flight if it was coming straight at you, but solid shot didn't need to actually hit anyone to cause damage. Because it was moving at nearly the speed of sound, its shock wave of compressed air—known as the wind of the ball—could burst blood vessels or even fracture bones in near misses. Even a spent ball rolling seemingly harmlessly along the ground was dangerous, carrying enough momentum that any show-off sticking his foot out to stop it could suffer crippling foot and leg injuries.

However frightful, solid shot was limited in its reach and impact. Scarier were the exploding shells fired by howitzers. Howitzers were specially designed to fire "bombs," hollow iron balls filled with gunpowder with a fuse ignited by the flash of firing. Howitzers were identified by their short barrels, usually made of brass and buffed to a high sheen by their proud gun crews. The comically short barrels were made that way for safety; the friction caused by exiting a full-length cannon barrel could make a bomb explode prematurely, so the howitzer traded range for safety, limiting its effective reach to 750 yards or so.

Handling these primitive exploding shells (one Major Henry Shrapnel would devise a more lethal version a few years later) was far from an exact science in 1776. Gunners had to tinker with the elevation and fuse length to get them to explode where they would cause the most harm. Air bursts over the heads of the enemy were the result to aim for; the metallurgy of the cast iron shells meant that they would fragment into large, jagged chunks, ensuring that there would be no slight wounds.

Preparing the assault with an hour-long bombardment of the American positions, the Hessian gunners found their range and inflicted serious damage, bringing the militia to the brink of panic. Colonel John Haslet of the Delaware Blues described it as "a continued peal of reiterated thunder," something a later century would term a drumfire barrage. Atop Chatterton Hill, Connecticut militiaman Elisha Bostwick later recalled the horror of that day: "Oh! What a sight that was to see within a distance of six rods those men with their legs and arms and guns and packs all in a heap."[32]

While the Hessian artillerymen zeroed in with Teutonic professionalism, the British cannoneers, by contrast, were of less use. They were firing from the lower elevation of Fisher Hill, and many of their balls overshot Chatterton Hill, while some fell short, bouncing down the steep slope to the consternation of the attacking columns struggling upward. The immense clouds of smoke thrown up by the ignition of gunpowder—the "fog of war"—further degraded targeting as time went on.

The thunder of the guns could be heard for miles, even reaching the far side of the Hudson River, where curious civilians gathered atop the Palisades to glimpse the rising smoke and speculate about what was going on.[33] Sheltered at Robbins Mills to the north, Abagail Purdy would have heard the guns, too, and wondered where her husband, Jacob, was in all that. Likewise, Ann Fisher Miller, like many other wives and mothers in the area, would have heard the distant roar, not knowing if her two sons were in harm's way.

The Americans on Chatterton Hill had little with which to reply. The point of attack was well out of range of the cannons in the American main line, and Washington committed only two pieces from the New York Artillery Company to back up the troops on Chatterton Hill. The commander of the artillery company was a bright young college kid by the name of Alexander Hamilton. Long-held belief (and historical depictions) has it that Hamilton personally commanded the guns on Chatterton Hill, though some historians have come to doubt whether he was actually present.[34] In any event, it was pointless to attempt counter-battery fire with a two-gun battery, so the cannons were parceled out to reinforce the infantry facing the British assault, where one of them was promptly disabled by a lucky shot from Fisher Hill.[35]

Having crossed the ford, the British and Hessians formed into columns for the climb up Chatterton Hill. Column formation, three or four abreast, minimized exposure to enemy fire while keeping the units in some sort of order when they reached the rim of the hill. Keeping soldiers together in formation was vital to ensuring the success of an assault; a disordered mass of men

Credited with defending Chatterton Hill, the young artillery captain Alexander Hamilton, shown here at the age of fifteen, three years before the war, became the youthful hero of the battle of White Plains. *Library of Congress.*

was more easily repulsed in the inevitable melee, and a column was better for breaking through a line of defenders and throwing *them* into disorder.

Speed was essential, but not everyone was willing to play by the book. Looking on from across the river, Howe and Clinton were dumbfounded by one officer who led his column halfway up the slope, only to halt his men while he took a leisurely potshot at the Americans. He then left his troops standing and taking casualties while he calmly reloaded for a second round. The officer responsible for this singular act of bravado was left unnamed in dispatches; he may have been killed by an American with no compunction about "shooting at brass."

In practice, shooting at brass was more like shooting at scarlet. The hand-tailored uniforms of British officers were made of a finer grade of fabric and a more costly dye than the coats of enlisted men. The resulting bright scarlet of the officers' coats thus stood out among the dull madder red the men wore, making officers easy to spot, even at a great distance. On a European battlefield, this was of little consequence; it was considered poor play to target enemy officers, and the men were actively discouraged from doing so. American soldiers, though, either hadn't read the rules or were happy to ignore them; as in other Revolutionary War battles, Chatterton Hill would produce a distressingly high proportion of British officer casualties.

From behind their cornstalk barricades, the Americans poured a murderous fire on the British and Hessians as they clambered uphill. Though all but useless for long-range targeting, at close range, the smoothbore musket was a devastating weapon. Its most effective killing zone began at fifty yards and only got better as the enemy advanced. Soldiers' wisdom had it that it took a man's weight in lead to kill an enemy soldier, but the Americans often enhanced their muskets' lethality by firing "buck and ball," a bullet (about the size of a marble) topped off with either four smaller pellets of buckshot or eight of bird shot, combining the musket's punch with the spread of a shotgun. One enterprising chap even fired balls with nails driven through their soft lead; the discovery of one of these spent rounds on the field prompted a formal protest from General Howe. British return fire was hampered by their column formation and by the tendency of men firing uphill to overshoot their targets.

The first British attempt on Chatterton Hill was thrown into disarray by American fire and bouncing British cannonballs, so the units were pulled back and reordered for a second attempt, which likewise came undone. Casualties were mounting, and Chatterton Hill was beginning to feel like another Bunker Hill as the British and Hessians regrouped for a third attempt.

At the northern end of the hill, the battleground's namesake, Michael Chatterton, and his family were caught in the middle of the conflict in more ways than one. Rather than flee, Michael, then at the advanced age of seventy-one, opted to shelter in place rather than leave his house open for one side or the other to loot. His home was located at the foot of the hill by the bridge, about where the "Welcome to Battle Hill" sign is today. Michael was a tenant farmer of Frederick Philipse and thus a signatory (perhaps by compulsion) of the Loyalist declaration signed at Hatfield's tavern, something that did not endear him to the local rebel militiamen. Nevertheless, he attended the same Presbyterian church as Abagail and Jacob Purdy and also owned land east of the Bronx River that he had purchased from members of their family. Years later, a patriotic family legend had it that Michael's wife, Mary, melted down her pewterware to cast bullets for the Americans, but being that Mary was four years deceased in 1776, this tale is unlikely. As the bullets (pewter or otherwise) began to fly, Michael, with his son William's family, sought refuge in the house's basement while British and Hessian cannonballs furrowed his hilltop cornfields.[36]

While the Hessians climbed the slopes of Chatterton Hill, another German was having his doubts about which side he had chosen. Born in Friesland, the lawyer Rudolphus Ritzema was colonel of the Third New York Regiment. Although he kept his men up to their task, Ritzema was deeply irked by a run-in he had had with his brigade commander, Lord Stirling, a few days before. Stirling had placed Ritzema on report for maintaining lax discipline in his unit, an odd thing considering that Ritzema was a veteran of the fiercely disciplined Prussian army. Forgetting that he was not in a courtroom, the argumentative lawyer confronted Lord Stirling, who promptly had him court-martialed for using disrespectful language with a superior officer. A disgruntled Ritzema would see the Battle of Chatterton Hill through but would defect to the British a few days later.

Though the militiamen were growing unsteady under the British bombardment, for the most part, the Americans on Chatterton Hill were not doing what the British hoped they would do: running like hell from the approach of the fearsome-looking grenadiers and brass-hatted Hessians. Having thrown two assaults into disarray, the militiamen and Continentals yet stood behind their cornstalks with loaded firelocks, awaiting another attempt. Not only were they not running away, but they were also not running out of ammunition as they had at Bunker Hill.

For the British and Hessians at Chatterton Hill, the topography of their approach was part of their problem. From his hillside perch at Hart's

Hessian colonel Johann Rall, here depicted as a marionette in a presentation commissioned by the Old Barracks Museum in Trenton, was a consummate soldier whose initiative secured a British victory on Chatterton Hill. *Photo by author; courtesy of Tom and Marianne Tucker, Tucker's Tales Puppet Theater.*

Corners, Johann Gottlieb Rall could plainly see that the British and Hessians were attacking up the steepest part of Chatterton Hill. The forty-year-old Colonel Rall (also spelled Rahl) was one of the more interesting personalities at the Battle of White Plains. A "soldier child," Rall had spent his entire life in the military and was a consummate soldier with a combat résumé as good or better than anyone on the field. Known for his energy and initiative, his reputation as a boozer and a playboy likely stemmed more from German stereotypes than from historical fact. Rall's initiative would make the difference for the British that day. When he was ordered into the attack, rather than charging straight ahead, Rall instead led his men westward on a long loop to the hill's gentler western slope. Sending the dragoons ahead to guard against a possible counterattack, Rall then brought his two infantry regiments from the west against the American left flank.

Advancing through late-season wheatfields set alight by errant musket sparks, Rall's attack staggered the Americans enough to permit the main British-Hessian force to finally crest the hill and form up for a fight on level ground. Caught between forces to the west and south, the American right flank was in a vise. They fell back to mount a defense from behind farmer Chatterton's stone walls. Their position atop the hill, though, was clearly untenable, and there was nothing to do but fall back farther to avoid being surrounded and overwhelmed. Once again, the task of holding off the enemy fell to the men from Delaware and Maryland.

The Maryland Regiment joined the Delaware Blues in slowing the British advance and allowing the remaining units on the hill to make an orderly withdrawal. Like the Delaware Blues, the Marylanders had joined the war as a fully uniformed and equipped unit—though unfortunately, their original state-issued uniforms were royal red livery. Knowing that this would cause confusion in battle against the King's regulars, the Marylanders accordingly swapped their red coats for the fringed linen hunting shirts that were the hallmark of the American rifleman. This at least helped make the enemy nervous, as in the redcoats' imagination, every man in a hunting shirt was a deadeye marksman—and indeed, the Maryland Regiment included a company of riflemen to maintain that impression.

The Marylanders had been something of a "silk stocking" regiment, composed of recruits from the leading families of Maryland society, who could be depended on at muster days to impress the onlookers (and marriageable young ladies) with their immaculate uniforms, polished accoutrements and precision drill. Some among them, such as the young Captain John Eager Howard, bore the names of more than one prominent

Maryland family (he would achieve the rare distinction of having three streets in his native Baltimore named in his honor: John, Eager and Howard).[37] Dismissive Loyalists would dub them "the Macaroni," but beneath the spit and polish, there was cold steel. Called to service, the Maryland Macaroni soon showed that they could fight. Along with the crisp uniforms, they had been issued bayonets and were well trained in their use.

The Marylanders were renowned for their heroic stalling of the British advance at the Battle of Brooklyn a few weeks before. Their counterattack at the Old Stone House by the Gowanus Creek enabled a portion of the American army to escape encirclement and capture, but their heroism cost them an appalling 256 men dead, wounded or missing, and the location of their mass burial site remains a Brooklyn mystery to this day. The Marylanders had replenished their ranks somewhat by the Battle of White Plains but were nevertheless a depleted shell of a once brilliant regiment. Called upon at Chatterton Hill to again cover an American retreat, they stood alongside the Delaware Blues and slowed the oncoming Hessians.

While the Marylanders had had to hastily change their uniform color, the blue coats of the Delaware men could also cause confusion, as in the haze of battle, they could be mistaken for the blue-garbed Hessians. There had already been a friendly fire incident the night after the Heathcote Hill fight, when a scouting party of Pennsylvania riflemen encountered a Delaware patrol. Nine Delaware Blues and six riflemen were killed in the ensuing firefight before things could be sorted out. Amid the "fog of war," as the attacking Hessians crested Chatterton Hill, they mistook the Delaware Blues for some of their own, prompting hasty orders to cease fire. Out of defiant unit pride, or perhaps a sense of gentlemanly sportsmanship, the Delaware men proudly announced their identity, and the shooting resumed.[38]

Backing up the Marylanders and Delaware Blues from behind a stone wall, the Dutchess County Militia also stood up to the fight, though their eventual retreat occasioned controversy when Adjutant General Joseph Reed accused Colonel Morris Graham of abandoning the position without orders and without even firing. At the ensuing court-martial, Graham's men testified that the colonel urged his men to stand and fight and did not retreat without orders. Graham was exonerated, but it remains unclear who, if anyone, actually ordered the retreat.

Among Graham's men was Andrew Frazier. Of mixed Scots and African ancestry, he was born in Morrisania in the present-day Bronx. It is uncertain whether he was born free or enslaved on what was then the estate of the Morris family, but at the outbreak of the war, he was a tenant farmer in Pine

The Delaware Blues joined the remnants of the Maryland Regiment to contest the assault on Chatterton Hill. *Photo by author.*

Plains in Dutchess County, on a newly settled tract of farmland known as the Little Nine Partners Patent. As a free man, Frazier served in the Patriot militia, taking an active part in raids and patrols. One of an untold number of men of color serving in the American forces, at White Plains, he was detailed as Colonel Graham's body servant, with the likely task of seeing to it that the colonel got off the field in one piece. Graham survived the fight, and Frazier would continue to serve in the war, eventually becoming a landowner in Pine Plains and dying in 1846, just short of his 103rd birthday.[39]

While the Maryland, Delaware and Dutchess County units slowed down the frontal assault from the southern end of Chatterton Hill, keeping the retreat's northern back door open was the job of Colonel Charles Webb, commanding the Nineteenth Continental Regiment at the left end of the American line. Webb ordered his Connecticut men to stand fast, and a belated British attempt to scurry up the north end of Chatterton Hill and cut off the American exit down the Dobbs Ferry Road was repulsed under the direction of young Captain William Hull, fighting in the vicinity of what today is the Battle of White Plains Park.

The "fog of war" was no mere figure of speech, as clouds of black powder smoke added to the confusion. *Photo by author.*

Webb's men would be the last American unit to exit Chatterton Hill, marching in good order down the Dobbs Ferry Road behind the Delaware and Maryland men and across the Chatterton Bridge to the safety of the forward American lines. To ensure their safe withdrawal, Washington directed Israel Putnam to detach men from Purdy Hill to cover their retreat. It wasn't necessary, though; the British were not coming after them. Generals Leslie and de Heister had been ordered to take Chatterton Hill, and they had done exactly that. The victorious Hessians and British stood in place atop the conquered cornfields, perhaps with a triumphant "hip, hip, huzzah," and advanced no farther. Howe issued no orders to pursue. It was now past three o'clock, with less than two hours of daylight remaining.

Chapter 7

GENERAL HOWE'S DILEMMA

T he chill light of dawn would reveal the limited nature of that victory. Howe had taken Chatterton Hill, for all the good it would do him. The threat to his left flank was indeed eliminated, but as a springboard for further action, Chatterton Hill itself left a lot to be desired. The Bronx River was still running high, and the Chatterton Bridge was still covered by Washington's guns on Purdy Hill. Even with the bridge secured, any attempt to maneuver around the rebel right flank would only encounter another set of hills with a narrow river valley between them—and assaulting the Americans from the west would mean crossing the river yet again, this time with no known fording places. Even though a flanking maneuver from Chatterton Hill was impracticable, it is nevertheless a mystery why Howe did not immediately order a general assault on Washington's main line.

The casualties the British and Hessians suffered in the taking of Chatterton Hill likely influenced Howe's thinking, and having observed the attack close at hand, Howe could see that the day had been a costly one. Casualty figures throughout the 1776 campaign are notoriously incomplete and unreliable, especially on the British side, as Hessian casualties were usually left unstated in reports to London. Estimates of the British and Hessian toll at Chatterton Hill run as high as 350 dead and wounded, though 200 may be closer to the mark. General Leslie reported 134 British casualties, and an additional 72 dead and wounded were reported for the Hessians, while incomplete American returns total 93.[40]

The Cannon Monument by the Bronx River Parkway sits at the base of Chatterton Hill near the Dobbs Ferry Road. Retreating Americans passed this spot after yielding the hill. *Photo by author.*

Even at the lower estimate, the butcher's bill was ghastly enough for such a secondary target, and Howe was now eyeing the American fortifications on Purdy and Hatfield Hills—hills nearly as high and steep as Chatterton Hill. The opposing forces being nearly equal (about thirteen thousand each), Howe put off ordering the main attack until additional reinforcements could be brought up from New York. The new attack date would be October 31, two days hence.

Unknown to either Howe or Washington, as the smoke cleared on Chatterton Hill, far-off events taking place that same day of October 28 would have a major impact on the progress of the war. Far to the north on Lake Champlain, General Sir Guy Carleton was eying Fort Ticonderoga and having his own doubts. Following the collapse of the 1775 American invasion of Canada, in the spring of 1776, he had led a British army into New York, intending to follow the time-honored Lake Champlain–Lake George–Hudson River invasion route and thereby break the United Colonies in two.

His opponent was the energetic Benedict Arnold, who, seeing that control of Lake Champlain was crucial to the success of Carleton's invasion, set about building a navy to contest British control of the waters, thereby forcing Carleton to halt and build his own lake flotilla. The boat building took up most of the summer, and by the time Carleton's flotilla defeated Arnold's squadron and secured possession of Lake Champlain at the Battles of Valcour Island on October 11 and Buttonmold Bay on October 13, the leaves were already off the trees, and the first snows of the approaching winter had fallen.

The Americans fell back and prepared to defend Fort Ticonderoga, which commanded the short portage between Lakes Champlain and George. Approaching Fort Ticonderoga, the British general became convinced (wrongly) that his invasion force was outnumbered by the fort's defenders. Concluding that the season was too far gone to risk getting mired in siege trenches at the end of an ice-choked Lake Champlain, Carleton ordered his men back to Canada to await the next year in safe winter quarters, and preparations for the pullout began on October 28. Howe, for his part, had given little concern to events on the northern front and would only learn of the invasion's failure in mid-November.

Meanwhile, far to the south at the mouth of the Delaware River, on October 28, Benjamin Franklin was embarking on a diplomatic mission to France that, the following year, would result in France's military alliance with the new nation, an alliance that would dramatically change the course of the war.

What should have been a decisive year, 1776, was petering out in disappointment for the British. William Howe's diffident direction of the campaign thus far puzzled his subordinates. Howe's behavior puzzled Parliament, too, and puzzles historians to this day.[41] The campaign admittedly had a late start due to the logistical delays of assembling a transatlantic army, but even so, exactly two months after the Battle of Brooklyn, the forces of the Crown had advanced less than forty miles and had still failed to break Washington's army, an army they had once dismissed as little more than a "rabble in arms."

Called before a formal inquiry by the House of Commons in the spring of 1779, Howe attempted to explain himself. Speaking from a prepared text to the assembled members of Parliament, he left out any mention of his altercation with General de Heister and would only say that "political reasons" caused him to hold back from launching a general assault at White Plains in the remaining daylight hours of October 28, 1776. Unclear about what Howe meant by "political reasons," the MPs called Howe's friend and onetime subordinate Charles, Earl Cornwallis, to give his perspective. Cornwallis, by nature an aggressive commander, could only say that he had no idea what those "political" reasons could have been. Parliament did not press the matter, and fearing embarrassment, His Majesty's Government quietly terminated the inquiry a few weeks later.[42]

The original draft of Howe's speech, discovered in 2010, sheds some light on what he was thinking at White Plains. De Heister's initial refusal to cross the Bronx River ford had shaken Howe's confidence in him, and even though the Hessians had gone on to storm Chatterton Hill, Howe remained unsure if he could depend on either de Heister or the Hessians in general. But in 1778, when the British were ever more dependent on their Hessian auxiliaries, it would have been impolitic to alienate them by speaking against them on the public record, so Howe left these thoughts unstated when he gave his speech. If Parliament had insisted on a fuller explanation, the draft indicates that Howe, speaking from hindsight, was prepared to say that an attack on Washington's lines would have done little strategic good, since the Americans would have been able to pull back to North Castle with little loss. But Parliament did not insist.

As night fell on October 28, Howe left his forces encamped on Chatterton Hill and the White Plains, where the nocturnal light of their campfires made an impressive sight for the Americans looking down from their brooding hills. Finding himself a commodious headquarters in Scarsdale at the Griffin house, which still stands today near the junction of the Post and Fenimore

SIR HENRY CLINTON.
From an English Print.

Howe's acerbic second-in-command, Henry Clinton, was tasked with planning the final assault on Washington's main line. *Benson Lossing,* Pictorial Field Book of the Revolution.

Roads, Howe conferred with his right-hand man, Henry Clinton, to consider their next move once the reinforcements arrived.

The de facto second-in-command of the British army, Henry Clinton was a curious counterpart to Charles Lee. Like Lee, Clinton was socially awkward and off-putting; in a moment of self-candor, he once described himself as a "shy bitch." Inclined to aggressive action, he was an odd subordinate to the slow-moving Howe, and he frequently chafed at his commander's lassitude. Though scrupulous in following orders once given, Henry Clinton was ever ready to offer contrary advice. At a loss for ideas, Howe now sought Clinton's input and asked him to reconnoiter the field and come up with a plan of attack.

Clinton did so, and on October 30 reported to Howe that, in his opinion, taking possession of a certain "bald hill" on the American right flank would pose a threat to the rebel position on Purdy Hill. The name and precise location of this bald hill are not specified in the surviving account. Clinton may have been thinking of Travis Hill across the river and northwest of Purdy Hill, whose broad crest is open ground to this day.[43] More likely, though, the hill Clinton had in mind was Juniper Hill, just north of Chatterton Hill, whose rocky prominence today overlooks the Tarrytown Road and the Westchester County Center.

Juniper Hill is a little over one thousand yards due west of Purdy Hill and thus closer to it than Chatterton Hill. Though it had a significantly lower elevation than Purdy Hill, if the British could position their cannons on Juniper Hill, Purdy Hill would be within their range. It was rather long range for howitzers but still doable. The Chatterton Bridge, though still within reach of the American cannons atop Purdy Hill, had not been destroyed, and Washington had pulled his men out of the forward line of entrenchments. A quick dash across the bridge would suffice to get the guns across the river and safely up the slope of Juniper Hill.[44]

Ever the contrarian, though, Clinton now found fault with the very plan he himself had just submitted. Artillery firing from his "bald hill," he argued, would only "stir" the Americans on Purdy Hill. Firing uphill

The Mortar Monument on North Broadway marks the site where, on November 1, Howe's assault troops found only empty trenches. *Photo by author.*

at long range, such a bombardment might have sufficed to knock the last of Abagail's apples off the trees, but it would not be enough to provoke a headlong retreat. Instead, he advised mounting purely diversionary assaults at either end of the American line, at Purdy and Merritt Hills. This would keep Washington from shifting his forces while the British launched their main thrust against the center of the American line where it crossed the York Road about a mile north of the White Plains village green. Although he had been dubious about the prospects of a general assault on Washington's main line, Clinton now felt that this approach—a double fake-out followed by a strong gut punch—had the best chance of success.

Howe may have been thinking the same thing himself. The center of the American line, along the York Road (present-day North Broadway), where the terrain made a dip between Purdy and Hatfield Hills, was arguably the most vulnerable point of the American defenses. The entrenchments there sat just below the crest of a long rise of ground, and a redoubt had been laid out but, for some reason, never constructed, leaving American defenses dependent on a single line of entrenchments. While assaulting troops would have to advance uphill across open terrain, it would be nothing like the mountaineering called for at Chatterton Hill—and certainly not anything that the British and Hessian grenadiers couldn't carry with a hearty huzzah and a swift bayonet rush.

It was a point of decision that could turn the stalled battle into a British victory. If Howe's forces could punch through there and gain command of the York Road, at the very least, they would complicate Washington's line of retreat; at best, they would split the American army in two, isolating Heath's forces on Hatfield Hill and making it feasible to destroy each segment in detail.

Washington himself, with his keen surveyor's eye for terrain, was aware of this danger and for that reason had personally taken command at the center. He was growing pessimistic about the vulnerability of this part of the line and was looking for an opportunity to fall back to a stronger position. "Our post," he wrote Congress on October 29, "from its situation, is not so advantageous as could be wished, and was only intended to be temporary and occasional, till the stores…could be removed."[45]

While Washington fretted, back at the Griffin house, Howe and Clinton could relax in the confidence that their plan was a sound one and that the arrival of the reinforcements the following day would ensure its success. Turning in for the night, they blew out the candles as the first raindrops spattered the windowpanes.

Chapter 8

THE DEFENSE OF MILLER HILL

L ate October in the Hudson Valley often brings spells of brilliant clear "leaf-peeping" weather, punctuated by days of hard, cold rain. Some autumns are wetter than others, and 1776 was one of those autumns. The rain that set in on the evening of October 30 was one of those fall soakers that sometimes come just in time to wash the leaves off the trees and spoil what remains of the leaf-viewing season.

Watching the rain pour down as day broke on October 31, Howe's concern wasn't the ruination of the fall scenery. The flintlock muskets of the day, with their spark-striking flints and their exposed priming pans that touched off the main charge, simply could not be made to fire in the rain—or even in excessively high humidity. Muddy ground, moreover, would absorb the force of the cannonballs, greatly reducing their destructive power against men and breastworks. Reluctantly, he postponed the attack until the rain could clear.

Some might have argued for going in anyway with a bayonet-only attack, something the British had long been masters of. Originally invented as a defense against cavalry, by 1776, the bayonet had evolved into a long, tapered, triangular blade designed for the sole purpose of stabbing infantrymen. Among Howe's junior officers, there were a number of bayonet enthusiasts. Dismissing the inaccurate musket as no more than a "good handle for a bayonet," they favored making attacks without pauses to exchange volleys, instead rushing in "with zeal and with bayonets only." One of these bayonet enthusiasts was Colonel Charles Grey, who, the following year, would earn the nickname of "No Flint" Grey for a gruesome nighttime all-bayonet assault at Paoli, Pennsylvania.

Bayonetting, though, was not a tactic for the squeamish, and Howe was too cautious to trust in cold steel alone. There was no need to hurry, not that Howe was ever in a hurry anyway. Washington was apparently going nowhere, so Howe left his men to shelter in their tents, leaving the battle to the next day.

Washington had other ideas that rain-lashed Halloween. He was anxious for an opportunity to pull back to the stronger hilltop positions Charles Lee had originally recommended, so for him, the rain was a providential cover for a midnight retreat. Following the nocturnal evacuation of Brooklyn a few weeks before, such midnight retreats were becoming part of Washington's tactical playbook, and he would reenact the same move a few weeks later after the Second Battle of Trenton, making possible the surprise attack and victory at Princeton. At White Plains, though, the object was simply survival.

For the men manning the trenches, some of whom were standing in ankle-deep water, the idea of a retreat would have been a welcome opportunity to be somewhere—anywhere—else than the muddy, rain-sodden ditches they had to occupy. "The water, before morning, was nearly over shoes," recalled Joseph Plumb Martin, "which caused many of us to take violent colds, by being exposed upon the wet ground after a profuse perspiration." Taken ill himself, Martin was sent to the rear but found little comfort there: "I had the canopy of heaven for my hospital, and the ground for my hammock." Luckily, fallen autumn leaves were plentiful, and Martin gathered a bunch of them to provide himself a sort of mattress.[46]

The rain cleared on the morning of November 1, and Howe could finally form up his troops for the big push. He had quietly dispensed with Clinton's recommendation for diversionary attacks and instead concentrated his forces for an assault up the York Road against the vulnerable center of the American defenses.

The American lines were strangely quiet, though, and the grenadiers received no fire as they advanced up the long slope toward the earthworks. Reaching the entrenchments, they found them empty. During the night, Washington had fallen back to the hills of North Castle, pivoting his forces to form a new line that ran from Miller Hill to Mount Misery, then across Foster Hill and on to Hatfield Hill, where Heath repositioned some of his troops to the north and west to form a continuous defensive line with the rest of the army.

The bleak stony terrain of Mount Misery was aptly named by American troops awaiting a British attack that never came. *Photo by author.*

By the standards of the eighteenth century, the moment Howe's men stepped across the entrenchments on the York Road, he could, having occupied the enemy's original line of battle, claim a technical victory. But the opportunity for a decisive stroke had been lost, and Howe knew it as he approached the new rebel line about a mile and a half to the north. There, the road ran through a narrow defile between the grim prominences of Miller Hill and Mount Misery, with the heights of Foster and Hatfield Hills glowering to the east and American gunmen positioned on top of each of them.

Confronting a rearranged battlefield, Howe was forced to make some uncharacteristically impromptu decisions. Hoping once again to catch the Americans in the flank and thereby force a retreat, Howe first attempted an attack around the eastern end of Horton's Pond. It was the scene of the abortive probe on Merritt Hill on October 28, but with General Heath having repositioned his troops to link up with the new American lines at North Castle, there was the possibility that a weakened defense on the eastern end of the line would permit a flanking move around Horton's Pond that

After a probe at Merritt Hill was rebuffed, Howe redeployed his troops to Miller Hill. *Photo by author.*

could gain the heights of Hatfield Hill and roll up the American lines from the south. It might have worked but for a last-minute decision by General Heath.

Inspecting his new line of battle early on the morning of November 1, Washington saw that Malcolm's Regiment was still occupying its original position across the pond on Merritt Hill and expressed his concern to Heath that the isolated unit might easily be overwhelmed and captured. Heath, at first, had been inclined to agree, fearful that a British force might weasel its way along the Mamaroneck River through the narrow valley separating Merritt Hill from Hatfield Hill and thereby isolate the Merritt Hill detachment. Heath issued orders to evacuate Merritt Hill, but being a New Englander with a fond eye for stone fences, he spotted a well-built wall that, if defended, would block any such maneuvers up the little valley. Deploying a regiment there, Heath quickly countermanded his evacuation order and left Malcomb's cannoneers to rake the British advancing against Merritt Hill. The accuracy of their fire quickly dissuaded the British from making any further advance, and the Second Battle of Merritt Hill proved to be another nonstarter.

Stymied in his eastern approach, Howe instead redeployed some of the troops assigned to the abortive Merritt Hill maneuver and prepared to attack the opposite end of the rebel line at Miller Hill and Mount Misery.

Mount Misery's name is said to have been bestowed on it by the shelterless soldiers who spent a chilly, rain-sodden night camped on its stony ground, lighting fires among the glacial boulders and trying to cook their diminishing supplies of flour into something resembling bread. It certainly was a miserable place to spend a rainy autumn night, but at a 440-foot elevation, Mount Misery was the highest of the area's hills, looming 80 feet above its neighboring Miller Hill. Its steep, rubble-strewn slopes offered no good line of approach for an attacking force, and Howe wisely decided to leave it alone and focus instead on Miller Hill.

Miller Hill was only slightly more approachable than Mount Misery, and moreover, it was held by John Glover's battle-wise brigade of New Englanders, the same men who had frustrated Howe's advance at Pell's Point two weeks earlier. Unlike the artillery-poor defense at Chatterton Hill, Glover had six fieldpieces atop Miller Hill, a mixture of three- and twelve-pounders and a single twenty-four-pounder. These he kept judiciously out of sight, waiting for the British to commit themselves to a line of attack.

Atop Miller Hill overlooking the Bronx River, Glover's men dug in to await the British attack. Their entrenchments may still be discerned today. *Photo by author.*

Facing the British for the second time in two weeks, Colonel John Glover, depicted on a statue in Boston, opened fire on the enemy deployed along the Bronx River. *Library of Congress.*

Still licking their wounds from Chatterton Hill, Alexander Leslie's brigade, including Rall's Hessians and the Forty-Second Highlanders, was detailed to once again mount an uphill assault, this time on Miller Hill. Avoiding Miller Hill's eastern slope, where they would be exposed to gunfire from neighboring Mount Misery, Leslie decided to hook around and attack up the western slope. Glover coolly watched Leslie's brigade as they deployed off the present-day Cemetery Road and picked their way through the marshes along the Bronx River. The westerly slope of Miller Hill was only slightly more climbable than the eastern side, and it was between the hill and a broad expanse of the river known as Willow Lake, meaning the British had a tight space in which to deploy.[47] As the British, Hessians and Scots arranged themselves for the attack, Glover unmasked his cannons and opened fire.

Glover's three- and twelve-pounders quickly wreaked havoc on the exposed assault troops. Colonel Laomi Baldwin, looking down from Miller Hill, noted that Glover's cannonade "soon made them run and scamper in the greatest confusion I ever saw." One American cannonball took the head off a Hessian artilleryman, perhaps providing the premise for one of Westchester's most enduring Halloween legends. Rall's Hessian brigade received fire from Glover's twenty-four-pounder, causing mounting casualties. With more than 150 men already dead and wounded in an attack that hadn't quite started, Leslie called a retreat.

The narrow space in which the British units were stacked up made it awkward to carry out an orderly withdrawal. The way west was blocked by Willow Lake, so the British had to retreat the way they came, falling back under flanking fire several hundred yards southward before they could cross the river and seek refuge on the comforting rise of Travis Hill. There, Leslie arranged his guns and began a brisk bombardment of Miller Hill. More than 1,000 yards from Miller Hill and at a 250-foot elevation, 100 feet lower, the British guns firing at Miller Hill from Travis Hill were at a significant disadvantage. Firing from a superior elevation, Glover's guns soon silenced them, and though shots would be exchanged over the next three days, the Battle of Miller Hill—and, with it, the Battle of White Plains—was essentially over.

Chapter 9

THE ARMIES DEPART

It is difficult to say whether, in his attacks on November 1, Howe was truly in earnest or was just making a demonstration to satisfy some sense of military honor or obligation. The attempts at Miller and Merritt Hills certainly showed that a general assault would only produce a bloodbath and a pointless one at that. The attempt having been made, Howe could with credibility break off the attack and pursue other options.

In any event, Howe could plainly see that Washington was unlikely to be going anywhere except to retreat farther north into the Hudson Highlands. As the retreating Americans posed no immediate threat to the British, it made little sense to chase after them. The British lacked detailed topographical maps of the inland area north of White Plains, and amid the increasingly rugged terrain, ambush and disaster could lurk behind any hill or turn in the road.

It was in fact wise for Howe to forego the pursuit. Even if, following Washington's route to Fishkill, the British gained the Pine's Bridge crossing over the Croton River before the Pyne brothers took the planks up again, an advance on Fishkill from the south would have run into another bottleneck at the Wiccopee Pass. There, the road ran through a narrow defile similar to that posed by Miller Hill and Mount Misery, and even if the British forced their way through the Wiccopee Pass, they would run up against yet more hilltop fortifications that were no doubt being constructed to defend the depot. Moreover, with winter rapidly coming on, the British commander would not want to stretch his fragile supply lines in a possibly fruitless chase after Washington.

Howe would, anyway, soon have another, more attractive objective. In his pullout from Manhattan, Washington had left behind the three thousand men garrisoning Fort Washington on the island's northern panhandle. This was not an oversight. Located at about the highest point of Manhattan Island, Fort Washington, together with Fort Lee on the New Jersey Palisades, bracketed the Hudson River. While the guns of the two forts were not able to interdict British navigation on the mile-wide river estuary, Fort Washington was nevertheless situated alongside the Kingsbridge Road, which led to the Harlem River crossings, the only landward route connecting New York City with the mainland. British possession of Manhattan Island, as well as the bridgeheads connecting the island with the mainland, would not be secure as long as the enemy held Fort Washington.

On November 2, the day after the abortive assaults on Miller and Merritt Hills, news came to Howe of a deserter from Fort Washington. The deserter, William Demont, was not just any soldier but an officer who had been the adjutant of the fort's commander, Colonel Robert Magraw. He brought the British detailed information revealing that Fort Washington was not as formidable as it seemed. The defenses were more of a disconnected series of outposts, and the central bastion, located on the site of today's Bennet Park in Washington Heights, was too small to hold the entire garrison. Moreover, it lacked a source of water; bucket details had to be sent downhill to draw water from a well at a tavern alongside Kingsbridge Road.

Knowing of Fort Washington's vulnerability, it made sense for Howe to leave off the unproductive Westchester campaign and bring his army back to Manhattan to take Fort Washington and consolidate his hold on the island. Washington could be left to his own devices, with a good chance that his army would fall apart by the end of the winter. In the meantime, Howe had to secure his own winter quarters in the partly ruined city of New York, and an excellent opportunity to do so had just been handed to him as if on a silver platter.

Howe had previously dispatched a Hessian brigade under Wilhelm von Knyphausen to probe the defenses at Fort Washington and tie down the rebels there. The same age as de Heister, to whom he was second-in-command of the Hessian forces, the more agreeable Knyphausen was becoming Howe's preferred Hessian. Knyphausen didn't have enough troops to storm the fort outright, but over the course of a week's reconnaissance, he acquired a detailed knowledge of the terrain, an invaluable addition to the information provided by the deserter Demont.

Taking Chatterton Hill had not been a useless expenditure of blood after all. Possessing the hill meant that the British now commanded the Bronx River crossing and the Dobbs Ferry Road and thus had the advantage of a direct route west to the Hudson, from which they could easily march down to Kingsbridge and prepare to deal with Fort Washington.

The Battle of White Plains thus far hadn't been much of a British triumph, but by maintaining a sense of continued forward motion, the seven-mile march to Dobbs Ferry from the conquered field of Chatterton Hill would at least preserve an appearance of victory. By presenting his army's flank and rear to the Americans, Howe's move might even tempt Washington to come down from the North Castle hills and offer battle on the more open terrain of Greenburgh.

Accordingly, given a due pause to prepare his marching orders, Howe slipped away from White Plains the night of November 4, leaving American observers to gaze down at the twinkling campfires that now warmed no soldiers. On the morning of November 5, it was the Americans' turn to wonder at the strange quiet on the fog-shrouded White Plains. Scouts, carefully probing the lines, discovered only a deserted British camp.

The notion of following Howe and hitting him in the flank or rear may have crossed Washington's mind, but his army was in no condition for an offensive. The state of his army's provisions was making him nervous; by November 1, he was already down to about five days' worth of flour, provided it was carefully rationed out. By November 5, the barrels were nearly empty, and the only sensible course was to remain in the Hudson Highlands and fall back toward his supply base at Fishkill.

Glover's artillery duel with British guns, on nearby Travis Hill, marked the last shots of the battle of White Plains. *Photo by author.*

Clothing was becoming a critical issue as well. In those days before durable synthetic materials, clothing was truly "organic" and became tattered when worn in the field for weeks on end. With many of them still wearing the same clothes they had on when they marched down from Boston seven months ago, the Americans were now "in so wretched a condition, as to clothing and accoutrements, that I believe no nation ever saw such a set of tatterdemalions," wrote one British officer. Observing the ragged condition of prisoners and deserters, he noted that "there are few coats among them but what are out at elbows, and in a whole regiment there is scarce a pair of breeches. Judge, then, how they must be pinched by a winter campaign."[48] Among his requests to Connecticut governor John Trumbull for food, Washington included an urgent plea to send clothing of any kind.

As the British marched away, a flaming act of vandalism would mar the moment of relief and mark an ash-strewn epilogue to the Battle of White Plains. Major Johnathan Austin of the Sixteenth Massachusetts had been among those probing the lines the morning of November 5 and discovering the British withdrawal. Blowing off two weeks' worth of accumulated tension, he and some of his men decided it was time to party. The disciplined British had left little behind worth scavenging, so they headed to Hatfield's and Oakley's taverns and set about drinking them dry. The men from Massachusetts had acquired a sour attitude toward the "Yorkers," whom they considered to be mostly a bunch of accursed Tories, and their liquor-stoked resentment erupted in a spate of looting and arson. Rampaging through the town, they torched the buildings of Loyalists and Patriots alike. The destruction included several homes, along with the courthouse, both taverns and the Presbyterian church.

Called to account for his unauthorized actions, Austin tried to claim that he burned the town in order to deny its use to the enemy. This was probably the worst thing to say, as it touched a sore point with Washington, who had been accused of doing the same thing to New York City a few weeks before. He had since then issued orders expressly forbidding any arson without specific orders from a general officer. Expressing his "astonishment and abhorrence," Washington had Austin quickly court-martialed and dismissed from the service.

With perhaps a wistful glance down the Dobbs Ferry Road, Washington now prepared for the next phase of his northward withdrawal. Retreating in the face of the enemy being the riskiest of military maneuvers, Washington waited until he was sure the British were well and truly gone before leaving White Plains on November 10.

The army would follow the route of its supply train north across the Croton River some fifty miles to Fishkill, where the new supply base was under construction. Buildings there were few, and space was tight; the Anglican Trinity Church and the local school building were pressed into service as hospitals for the sick and wounded who were able to make the journey from White Plains, while the stone-built Dutch Reformed church served as a makeshift guardhouse and jail. Barrels of provisions were stored anywhere that was sheltered from the rain; the soldiers made do as best they could while barracks were under construction.

The more severely wounded were left at a field hospital set up at St. George's Church in Mount Kisco, about ten miles north of White Plains. The Reverend Ephraim Avery, parson of St. George's, wasn't there to object; a declared Loyalist who, until recently, had been calling upon his Anglican congregants to pray for King George, he had lately turned up in Rye, lying dead with his throat cut, possibly by the hand of an irate rebel.[49]

The wounded who sheltered in the church, mostly casualties from Chatterton Hill, fared little better than the assassinated parson. The ten-mile ride over a road deeply rutted by supply wagons would have been an agony for men suffering from severe wounds and shattered limbs. Once there, there was little the medical knowledge of the day could do for them. Army physicians and nurses, many drawn from among the female camp followers, cared for them to the best of their abilities, but all too often, in an age lacking antiseptics or internal surgery techniques, it was not enough. Suffering from shock, tetanus, gangrene, peritonitis or internal hemorrhaging, many died in care and were buried in a corner of the churchyard.

Like many of his fellow soldiers, Corporal Jacob Patch knew that field hospitals were places best avoided if at all possible. His brother Simon was severely wounded in the thigh at Chatterton Hill. Jacob somehow got him off the hill, but rather than leave him to the dubious medical ministrations at Mount Kisco, Jacob got hold of a horse and rigged up a sort of litter. Threading sapling poles through the saddle stirrups, he placed Simon on a bale of hay and set off on the two-hundred-mile journey to their home in Groton, Massachusetts. His brotherly effort would prove to be in vain; Simon died at home a few weeks later on December 31.[50]

Untroubled by any pursuit by the tattered rebels, Howe marched his men across to Dobbs Ferry and down present-day Broadway to Kings Bridge. Howe found himself a new headquarters by the Bronx River, in the home of Elizabeth Delancey at West Farms. The widow of Peter Delancey, who owned a profitable set of water-powered mills along the river, Elizabeth was

American casualties of Chatterton Hill are buried at the site of a field hospital in Mount Kisco. *Photo by author.*

an avowed Loyalist who had gone so far as to name her mansion Union Hill. Of Huguenot origins, the Delanceys were a well-established and politically connected merchant family with extensive holdings both at West Farms and in Manhattan, and the well-furnished Union Hill, set on a bluff overlooking the river, was as welcoming and commodious a field headquarters as any

Howe would find himself in. There, he and Clinton sat down to devise a plan for the fall of Fort Washington.

To take the Fort, Howe would have to shake off his aversion to attacking hilltop entrenchments. Taking no chances, Howe and Clinton plotted a converging three-pronged assault that would envelope the fort from multiple directions. The attack, in which Johann Rall once again distinguished himself, forced the surrender of Fort Washington on November 16. Four days later, George Cornwallis led a force across the Hudson River and climbed a narrow road up the palisades, prompting the abandonment of Fort Lee without a shot being fired. The focus of the war now switched to New Jersey, marking the beginning of Washington's long "retreat to victory" that would culminate at Trenton.

Chapter 10

AFTERMATH

With the season's first frosts dusting the now quiet fields, White Plains' civilians and militiamen returned to what was left of their homes to resume their lives, acutely aware that, although the armies had departed, they were not out of danger. As the British settled into New York City and the Americans hunkered down far to the north in Fishkill, central Westchester became part of a "neutral ground," or a no-man's-land between the contending armies.

Free-ranging bandits and self-professed adherents to either side were already plaguing the county, and their depredations would only grow worse as the war continued. Loyalist "Cowboys" led by the former county sheriff James Delancey would gallop forth from West Farms to range throughout the Bronx River valley in search of Patriot cattle that they could sell to the British army, while ostensibly pro-independence "Skinners" robbed and trashed Loyalist homesteads, earning a name for themselves by going so far as to "skin" the wallpaper off the walls.[51] A variety of spies and secret agents would also haunt the neutral ground, making it difficult to trust any itinerant cobbler or peddler.

Some thrifty farmers found innovative ways of recycling the detritus of war. Story has it that one fellow in Greenburgh scavenged the field at Chatterton Hill for spent musket balls. Pounding flat the soft lead bullets, he fashioned them into a floor for his smokehouse.[52] Returning from his militia duty, Daniel Hatfield is said to have gathered up iron cannonballs that he used to provide a base for a fireplace in his new home near Horton's Pond.[53]

Among the battle's detritus were the bodies of dead soldiers. In those days before grave registration teams, the burial of the fallen was largely left to chance. Young British captain William Glanville Evelyn, mortally wounded at the Battle of Pell's Point, died in Manhattan on November 6 and was buried with full honors in Trinity Churchyard. Others would not receive the same attention.

Hessian dead at Chatterton Hill were casually buried on the field or left where they lay; some of their remains would be turned up when the Americans returned to occupy the hill in 1778, to the shock and surprise of Joseph Plumb Martin. Local rumor had it that additional remains were found amid the development of the Battle Hill neighborhood in the 1920s. Several American dead were buried at the White Plains Presbyterian Church, possibly along with an unknown number of British. Hessian and American casualties from the Battle of Pell's Point who died at St. Paul's Church in Eastchester were likewise buried in the surrounding churchyard in communal graves, where they are today honored in an annual commemorative ceremony.

Located on the edge of town, Abagail Purdy's home had escaped both British cannonballs and the torch of Major Austin. Her husband, Jacob, had survived his militia duty, and together, they resumed their modest lives as farmers. Getting through the winter would be a challenge, but ere long, it would be time to again sow the wheatfields, and the apple blossoms would once more brighten the trees on Purdy Hill.

Ann Fisher Miller returned to her home to find that General Charles Lee had been a truly horrid houseguest. In her absence, he'd taken a fancy to some of her curtains and thought they'd make a nice lining for his cloak. Ann's friend Sarah Mott, who had made the curtains herself, happened by Ann's house to find Lee's tailor squatting on the floor about to trim her curtains into a cloak lining, and Lee was completely unapologetic about it. Sarah succeeded in reclaiming the curtains, and Ann appears to have made no formal complaint. She had come through the battle better than many people in the area; as far as she knew, her two sons were alive and marching with their regiment to Fishkill, and her home, apart from broken furniture, was still intact.[54]

Ann, though, would again be grief-stricken when, just before Christmas, news arrived that her two sons John and Elijah Jr. had died in camp at Fishkill on December 21. At some point, they had been transferred from Drake's Third Regiment of Westchester Militia to the Fifth Continental Regiment. Their cause of death was listed simply as "fever," possibly typhus or typhoid; both were common camp diseases of the age, and the Fishkill cantonment was already acquiring a reputation as a notoriously unhealthy place. Ann was able to have their bodies brought back from Fishkill, and they were buried alongside their father in the White Plains Presbyterian churchyard.

Ann Fisher Miller would have another brush with history two years later, when Charles Lee returned to her house, this time in disgrace.

Captured at a tavern in Basking Ridge, New Jersey, on December 18, Lee returned to the American army in a prisoner exchange early in 1778 and resumed his command. His questionable actions at the Battle of Monmouth on June 30, 1778, led to his court-martial, the last sessions of which were almost certainly held at the Miller house when the American army returned to the White Plains

Captured a few weeks after the battle and later exchanged, Charles Lee returned to the Miller House in 1778 to face a court-martial. *Library of Congress.*

area. Ann thus saw not only Charles Lee again cross her threshold but also thirteen high-ranking Continental officers who comprised the court-martial panel. In addition, Ann briefly hosted General Horatio Gates, fresh from his victory at the Battle of Saratoga and on the way to his own disgrace at the Battle of Camden two years later, as well as General Alexander McDougall, who had commanded the American forces at Chatterton Hill. Concluding the court-martial, Charles Lee was convicted and sentenced to be suspended from command for one year. In a huff, Lee exited Ann's house—and the stage of American history—for good.[55]

Ann continued to maintain the farm with her remaining son and became an early adherent of the new Methodist denomination, opening her home to host their first meetings in the White Plains/North Castle area. Having lost her husband and two of her sons to the cause of independence and twice hosted the American high command in her home, she would live to the age of ninety-one and be buried alongside her husband and sons in 1819. The location of her grave became uncertain after her tombstone went missing early in the twentieth century, but in 2015, historians Cynthia Kauffman and Debra Palazzo confirmed her burial site and saw to the erection of a new tombstone carved in an appropriate eighteenth-century style.

Abagail Purdy would also have another encounter with history. Keeping a judicious distance from the court-martial of Charles Lee at the Miller house, George Washington returned to the Purdy homestead to establish his headquarters in the summer and autumn of 1778. Amid the comings and goings of various officers, another notable figure would cross Abagail's doorstep. Prowling the American camps in the guise of a poor widow peddler named "Mrs. Barnes," the Loyalist spy Ann Bates would twice gain entrance to the Purdy house, once lingering long enough to get a glimpse of George Washington. Never apprehended as a spy, the unassuming Ann was able to return to New York City and confirm the location of Washington's headquarters, along with a detailed account of the men and guns stationed at White Plains.[56]

Abagail and Jacob continued to live on their farm and served as prominent members of the Presbyterian Church of White Plains. After briefly hosting General Washington one more time in 1781, they both lived to an advanced age; Jacob died in 1822, and Abagail lived on to 1839, long enough to apply for a Revolutionary War widow's pension shortly before her passing. Abagail and Jacob Purdy are buried alongside each other in the Presbyterian churchyard.

The end of the war did not close the rifts in the extended Purdy family. Jacob's brother Gabriel, along with a number of other Purdys and Loyalist members of other local families, left the new United States for refuge in British Canada at the close of the war. Obtaining a land grant in Cumberland County, Nova Scotia, this band of Westchester Loyalists established a community in what they duly named the Westchester Valley, and a Westchester Station remains on the map to this day, along with a Purdy Lane and a Purdy Cemetery. The Loyalist Purdys flourished in their new home, some attaining prominent positions in government and business, as evidenced by the Purdy Wharf in the port city of Halifax.[57]

The Loyalist Michael Chatterton remained on his farm. Like other families in White Plains, Chatterton's family split up after the war, with some opting to remove to Canada. A namesake of his, a Michael Chatterton and his family, is listed among the passengers on the transport ship *Grace* en route to new lives in St. John's, Nova Scotia. The senior Michael Chatterton lived on to about 1785. His hilltop farm, though, remained the property of the Loyalist Frederick Philipse and thus liable to seizure and sale by the newly established State of New York. Perhaps with the understanding that he had been a reluctant Loyalist, the New York Commissioners of Forfeitures didn't get around to officially seizing Michael's house and cornfields until a year after his death, even though they were by then occupied by his son William. The farm was nevertheless sold to James Nelson in May 1786, but the name of Chatterton Hill would remain on the map for another 150 years.[58]

Johann Rall's star rose after White Plains, only to be abruptly snuffed out. At the assault on Fort Washington, Rall and his Hessian brigade were assigned the most difficult line of approach, attacking from the north up a steep slope to storm the outlying American works at Fort Tryon. (The terrain, rising from today's Dyckman Street to the site of the Cloisters Museum, remains little changed today.) Rall's bold ascent gained him the admiring sobriquet of "the Lion," and when the British finished their advance to the Delaware River a few weeks later, Rall's brigade was chosen to garrison the town of Trenton.

By now openly contemptuous of the Americans, Rall failed to fortify his position, and on the day after Christmas, Washington's army swept in out of a sleet storm to kill or capture over one thousand Hessians. Rall was mortally wounded trying to rally his men. Shortly before his death, he was surprised to learn that the German-speaking interpreter brought in to interview him was a long-lost cousin of his. Rall and over one hundred of his soldiers were buried in the nearby Presbyterian churchyard. The site is now covered by a parking lot, but reenactors honor his memory with a formal salute every year on or about the anniversary of the Battle of Trenton.

Leopold Philip de Heister's military career was a collateral casualty of the Battle of Trenton. With Rall dead, de Heister was designated the disaster's fall guy by General Howe, who by this point was no doubt happy for the excuse to get rid of him. De Heister was replaced by his own second-in-command, the more compliant Wilhelm von Knyphausen. A broken-hearted de Heister returned to Hesse-Cassel and died less than a year later.

Shortly after the Battle of White Plains, General William Howe was knighted Sir William as a reward for his exploits, such as they were. After the disappointing outcome of the 1777 campaign, he resigned his command, complaining of lack of support from both the London administration and from American Loyalists. Led by Major John André, his officers saw him off with a legendary blowout party named the Mischianza. Sir William sailed for England from Philadelphia in May 1778 and survived a Parliamentary inquiry into his conduct during the war. His acerbic subordinate Henry Clinton now found himself commander in chief, only to be dogged by troop cuts as the French entry into the war expanded it into a global conflict.

John Haslet commanded his Delaware Blues through the soul-trying times of Washington's retreat to the Delaware and recrossed the river to

Two months after White Plains, Johann Rall was killed when American troops stormed Trenton, New Jersey. Present-day reenactors fire a formal salute to Rall and his men at their burial place in downtown Trenton. *Photo by author.*

take part in the turnabout victory at Trenton, only to be killed at the Battle of Princeton on January 3, 1777. Learning of Haslet's death, Washington was reportedly brought to tears. By now the once powerful Delaware Regiment was reduced to a mere ninety-two men, most of whom chose to return home when their enlistments were up after the Battle of Princeton. The remaining handful of Blue Hen's Chickens were absorbed into the Maryland Regiment.

Carrying on after their embarrassing night on Heathcote Hill, the Queen's Rangers received a new commander the following year. Tasked with defending the fortifications above Kingsbridge in the face of an attack by General Heath in January 1777, Robert Rogers led his outnumbered rangers out of their trenches in a bold counterattack that scattered the Americans. His action, though, was deemed reckless and in violation of his orders, and Colonel Rogers was relieved of command. After a brief stint leading a unit of "King's Rangers" in Nova Scotia, Rogers died in obscurity in London. The new commander of the Queen's Rangers, John Graves Simcoe, would reshape the dispirited band into a mounted force that would return to Westchester as one of the most feared and ruthless units in the British army.

The turncoat colonel Rudolphus Ritzema accepted a British commission as a lieutenant colonel but never found a significant role to play in the war. His chief contribution to the cause of King George was the raising of a short-lived Loyalist unit with the odd title of the Royal American Reformers. Never brought to account for his desertion, Ritzema ended his days in Devon, England, as a half-pay retired officer.

William Hull, who distinguished himself by repelling the British attempt to cut off the retreat from Chatterton Hill, continued to serve throughout the war and eventually rose to the rank of lieutenant colonel. A friend of the unfortunate Nathan Hale, Hull is credited with publicizing Hale's reputed quote, "I regret that I have but one life to give for my country." As a brigadier general in the War of 1812, he was court-martialed for the surrender of Detroit and sentenced to death by firing squad, only to be reprieved by President James Madison.

Though his presence at Chatterton Hill has been disputed, in popular memory, Alexander Hamilton became the youthful hero of the Battle of White Plains. If his actions at White Plains did not bring him to the attention of his superiors, his handling of the artillery on the long retreat through New Jersey and at the victorious Battle of Princeton certainly did, and in March 1777, just four months after the Battle of White Plains, he became an aide to General Washington. He went on to become a valued member of Washington's staff and, after the war, one of the new nation's founders, coauthoring *The Federalist Papers* and serving as the first secretary of the treasury, only to die in a duel with his fellow White Plains veteran Aaron Burr in 1804.

Joseph Plumb Martin reenlisted in a Continental regiment and served to the end of the war. In 1830, he published his memoirs, *A Narrative of Some of the Adventures, Dangers, and Sufferings of a Revolutionary Soldier*. The book fell into obscurity, only to be rediscovered in 1962, republished as *Private Yankee Doodle* and hailed as a rare "rank and file" view of the Revolutionary War. It has been in continuous publication ever since. Joseph Plumb Martin heard one final volley in 1836, when a platoon of U.S. light infantry, passing through his hometown of Milford, Connecticut, paused at Martin's house to fire a formal salute to the old veteran.

Chapter 11

REMEMBRANCE

Though it has often been given short shrift in histories of the Revolutionary War, there have been a number of efforts over the years to memorialize the Battle of White Plains.

In 1877, the New York State Legislature passed an act incorporating the Battle of White Plains Monument Association, whose mission was "to provide for the laying out of a plot of ground in the village of White Plains… and for the erection of a monument thereon, commemorating the battle of White Plains."

Marking the centennial of the battle the year before, the association had already organized the ceremonial laying of a cornerstone for the proposed monument on Chatterton Hill. As the centennial faded into old news, the initiative faltered, and the intended obelisk was never built. The location and fate of the cornerstone remains unclear.

In 1926, the sesquicentennial, or 150th anniversary of independence, brought renewed interest in the Battle of White Plains. The local-born artist Edmund F. Ward painted a dramatic mural of defiant American cannoneers on Chatterton Hill that became the basis of a two-cent commemorative stamp issued that year. Originally hung in the White Plains Post Office, the mural was restored and moved to the White Plains Public Library in 1984. The painting has the unofficial title of *Hamilton at the Cannon*, though Ward insisted his intention was only to paint a typical gun crew. Asked about it later, Ward made it plain that "I didn't paint Hamilton. I didn't want Hamilton."[59]

The year 1926 also saw a commemoration coupled with a rather odd reenactment of the battle on Chatterton Hill. Organizers engaged the U.S. Army to participate, and the army, eager to promote the purchase of armored fighting vehicles to a budget-stingy Congress and public, brought in a squadron of "Whippet" tanks. Deploying on Michael Chatterton's old cornfields, the Whippets proceeded to knock over some of the remaining stone walls on the battlefield. Cynics held that this was done in cahoots with the developers of the newly named Battle Hill Park neighborhood to clear the field for development.[60] The name of Chatterton Hill itself became a casualty of development: the new upscale neighborhood would henceforth be known as Battle Hill and its portion of the old Dobbs Ferry Road redesignated Battle Avenue.

With the cooperation of the new Bronx River Parkway Commission, a monument was nevertheless erected: the "Cannon Monument" was installed beside the old Dobbs Ferry Road at the bottom of Chatterton Hill in 1926, linking the two phases of the battle by mounting the cannon on a boulder brought down from Mount Misery and pointing it downstream toward where the British and Hessians forded the Bronx River. Displaying an original cannon barrel from the battle, the Cannon Monument would suffer its own troubles over the years. The cannon was stolen in 1963 but recovered, only to be stolen again in 1971, this time for good. The Cannon Monument was eventually restored with a reproduction gun and today greets motorists approaching White Plains on the Bronx River Parkway.

A mile away from the Cannon Monument, another battlefield relic would mark a critical part of the field. Sporting a mortar left behind in the mud by Washington's retreating soldiers, over on North Broadway, the "Mortar Monument" marks the point where Washington's entrenchments crossed the York Road. A faint trace of these entrenchments may still be discerned there today. Another monument sporting a cannon was erected at the site of Merritt Hill at the far eastern end of the American lines.

Still another cannon would grace Battle Hill for a number of years. In 1915, a deck gun from the sunken USS *Maine* was donated to White Plains and set up on a granite base in Whitney Park to mark the purported site where Alexander Hamilton manned his two-gun battery. The gun was anachronistic and the location erroneous, and after much vandalism, it was removed in 2002, to be eventually remounted on the Veterans Memorial situated on the old White Plains village green on North Broadway.

Whippet tanks notwithstanding, Congress in 1926 proclaimed a White Plains National Battlefield Site but appropriated no funds with which to

Left: Chatterton Hill is, today, an upscale neighborhood in White Plains known as Battle Hill. *Photo by author.*

Right: The signposted Heritage Trail in White Plains links the main sites associated with the battle. *Photo by author.*

purchase land for it. The project faltered into the Depression, and plans for the stillborn national battlefield were transferred to the National Park Service (NPS) in 1933. The NPS was authorized to develop it as a national park, but again, no funds were appropriated, and the NPS finally dropped it for good in 1956.

At this point, historically minded local people came together to revive the idea of building a monument to the battle. The Battle of White Plains Monument Committee was organized in 1958. The committee researched existing buildings and sites associated with the events of 1776 and gathered them into an eleven-mile-long signposted heritage trail. The trail's red, white and blue wayfinding markers may still be seen mounted on telephone poles along the route, even though some of its sites, such as General Heath's headquarters at the Gilbert Hatfield house, have fallen to decay and development. The trail was remapped by Boy Scouts Troop X of White Plains in 2010, which also offers a Heritage Trail Patch to intrepid scouts who hike the entire length of it on foot.

A major success of the monument committee was the rescue of the Jacob Purdy House. The early 1960s was the heyday of an "urban renewal" movement eager to bulldoze historic streetscapes, and the Purdy home was one of a number of tattered old buildings along Spring and Water Streets that were slated for demolition. In 1962, the committee was able to get the house moved out of harm's way to a newly created park at the crest of Purdy Hill—no small feat, considering the steepness of that hill. Today, the restored Purdy House is the headquarters of the White Plains Historical Society (organized as the successor to the monument committee in 1983), and together with the Elijah Miller House, the Purdy House gives White Plains the rare distinction of having two extant "Washington's Headquarters."

This duality prompted some controversy as to which of the two houses was truly Washington's headquarters during the Battle of White Plains. Noting the dangerously forward position the Purdy House would have occupied once the British showed up, the Daughters of the American Revolution held forth for the Miller House and saw to it that a "Washington's Headquarters" sign pointing to the Miller House was set up by the Bronx River Parkway's Virginia Road exit. The White Plains Historical Society maintained that the Purdy House should share the honor. Scholarly research and a spirit of historical congeniality brought about a consensus in the mid-1980s that Washington likely occupied the Purdy House for a brief period in October 1776 before moving to the Miller House and certainly headquartered in the Purdy House for a longer stay in 1778.[61]

After serving as a historic site for nearly a century, the Miller House fell into neglect and decay in the early years of the twenty-first century, reaching a state almost beyond salvage. Local citizens and historians fended off proposals to demolish it or relocate it to the Kensico Dam Plaza or, like the Purdy House, to haul it uphill to the park at the top of Miller Hill. Following years of discussion with the Daughters of Liberty's Legacy and the Friends of the Miller House/Washington's Headquarters, Westchester County came through with the funds to restore it, and the Miller House was reopened at its original location in 2019.

The 1976 bicentennial brought a renewed wave of interest in the Revolution, and in White Plains, this was marked by the redesign of the old Whitney Park into a new Battle of White Plains Park atop what is now known as Battle Hill. This small park is distinguished by a wealth of informational signboards installed for the 225th anniversary of the battle in 2001 and was refurbished and rededicated in 2015.

For many years throughout the 1950s, 1960s and 1970s, an annual reenactment event was held on the field at the Merritt Hill monument at Silver Lake. The area fell into neglect until local historian Alex Funicello

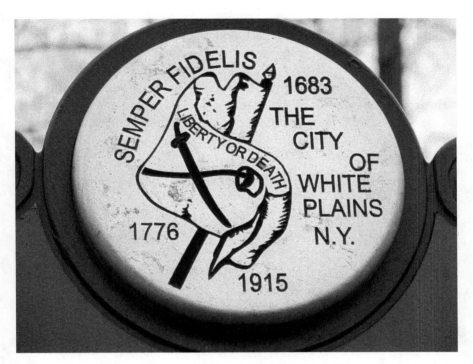

With its defiant "Liberty or Death" motto, the White Plains Battle Flag emblazons the city's seal. *Photo by author.*

organized and funded its refurbishment in time for the 225th anniversary. Fondly remembering the reenactments he saw there as a child (which had been discontinued due to the lack of parking), he organized a modest reenactment at the site for the 226th anniversary in 2002.

In 2001, the living history organization the Brigade of the American Revolution embarked on an ambitious recreation of the entire 1776 campaign in New York and New Jersey, with battles reenacted as much as possible in real time and at the original locations. White Plains, though, no longer had the open space to host the weekend-long encampments of hundreds of reenactors, so the assault on Chatterton Hill was recreated on a hillside in Ward Pound Ridge Reservation in northern Westchester. The White Plains Historical Society and the Second New York Regiment, Brigade of the American Revolution, continue to hold a commemorative living history event at the Purdy House for the battle's anniversary in late October each year, and the St. Paul's Church National Historic Site in Mount Vernon also holds a similar annual event commemorating the Battle of Pell's Point.

Believed to have been a militia flag flown at the battle, the red-fielded "Battle of White Plains Flag," with its defiant inscription of "Liberty or Death," became the centerpiece of the civic seal when White Plains was incorporated as a city in 1915. Today, it is flown at reenactments and historical commemorations, emblazons signboards and municipal property and serves as a proud reminder of a crucial week in October 1776 in which the American Revolution might have been lost but instead was preserved at White Plains.

Notes

Chapter 1

1. Also spelled "von Heister," though he tended to use the French article "de."

Chapter 2

2. The King's Bridge crossed present-day West 230th Street, carrying the Boston Post Road northward to the mainland. A second bridge, variously known as the Farmer's Bridge, Free Bridge or Dyckman Bridge, crossed the Harlem River eastward, connecting with present-day Fordham Road in the Bronx. The British would later add a pontoon bridge south of the Farmer's Bridge.
3. The bridge and causeway were approximately on the line of East Tremont Avenue in present-day Westchester Square. The upper reaches of Westchester Creek were landfilled early in the twentieth century.

Chapter 3

4. Barr, *Ancient Town of Pelham*, 83. The Wading Place was at the crossing of present-day Colonial Avenue; the bridge was at today's South Fulton Avenue, Mount Vernon.

5. Split Rock Road was, in fact, an old Indian trail, but this tale, like a number of other ghostly legends in the area, has no basis in fact.

6. Poirer, "Legacy of Integration." The Loyalist Queen's Rangers, under John Graves Simcoe, would be an exception to segregation, and curiously, some Hessian units would eventually recruit African Americans, usually as musicians.

7. Bell, "Evidence." Additional evidence that the fighting began at Glover's Rock was several cannonballs dug up in the vicinity at the beginning of the twentieth century. See Sanborn, *Gen. John Glover*, 5. An archaeological dig in 1980 also turned up a piece of grapeshot.

8. Bell, "Cannonball Fired." The location of the find on Prospect Hill suggests it was a shot fired by the Americans.

9. Casualty figures from the Battle of Pell's Point have been debated over the years. Deserters from the British side reported eight hundred to one thousand casualties, with two hundred dead, figures that would have made Pell's Point a bloodbath on the scale of Bunker Hill. American army headquarters eventually claimed five hundred, but Howe reported only four dead and twenty-one wounded (albeit not counting Hessians). For the British, the cost of Pell's Point was not so much measured in blood but in time and momentum.

Chapter 4

10. Scharf, *History of Westchester County*, 439.
11. Burdick, "Delaware's Colonel John Haslet."
12. Ewald, *Diary of the American War*, 8.

Chapter 5

13. Boyle, "James McMichael Journal."
14. Hatfield, *Hatfields of Westchester*.
15. Collins, *Enoch Crosby*, 101.
16. Ibid., 67.
17. The Fishkill base was not entirely secure; it would suffer a devastating British raid in 1777.
18. Peter Henderson, *Campaign of Chaos*, 450.

19. McDonald and Seymour, *McDonald Papers*, 73.
20. Elijah's unit, known as Drake's Regiment, constructed and occupied the fortification at Horn's Hook overlooking the Hell Gate, on the approximate site of today's Gracie Mansion. I have not identified any action taking place on August 21 at or around Horn's Hook. Elijah might have been wounded in the British bombardment of the fort on August 28 or 29.
21. Kriss, "Rediscovery of Silver Lake."
22. Stirling Forest in New York's iron-rich Ramapo Mountains is named for him.
23. His name is commemorated by Greenwich Village's iconic McDougall Street.

Chapter 6

24. McDonald and Seymour, *McDonald Papers*, 70.
25. Scharf, *History of Westchester County*, 436.
26. Martin, *Narrative*, 40.
27. The Sauthier-Faden Map (London, 1777), based on information gathered by Claude-Joseph Sauthier, a Swiss engineer accompanying the British army, and considered the most detailed map of the New York campaign, depicts a deeper westerly bend of the river at the foot of Chatterton Hill, and the low terrain there today makes this plausible.
28. McDonald and Seymour, *McDonald Papers*, 72.
29. The "Hessian bridge" is one of the more uncertain details of the battle; it is not included in all accounts, though Joseph Plumb Martin recalled it (Martin, *Narrative*, 40). In the context of de Heister's reluctance to immediately send his men into the ford, an attempt to improvise an alternative crossing makes sense.
30. McDonald and Seymour, *McDonald Papers*, 74.
31. Lederer, *Place Names*, 158.
32. Powell, "Connecticut Soldier," 94.
33. Henderson, *Campaign of Chaos*, 469.
34. Scharf, *History of Westchester County*, 441. Surviving records of the battle do not mention him; the first account of him being on Chatterton Hill is from the biography written by his son after his death and may be based on a misattributed quote. Hamilton was apparently stationed on the left-center of the American line under General Heath and thus saw no action during the battle. See Schenawolf, "Alexander Hamilton."

35. Scharf, *History of Westchester County*, 443.
36. Kennedy, *James Lawless, Jr.*, 93.
37. Fanelli, "One Famous, One Forgotten."
38. Burdick, "Colonel John Haslet."
39. Jago et al., "Rhinebeck's Lost and Found".

Chapter 7

40. Scharf, *History of Westchester County*, 446.
41. Scurrilous gossip at the time (and repeated in some histories) had it that Howe was distracted by an affair he was having with Elizabeth Loring. There is little evidence to support this and much reason to doubt this affair ever took place. See Flavell, *Howe Dynasty*, 289–91.
42. Smith, *Whispers across the Atlantick*, 139.
43. The name of Travis Hill may date from after the war, when Uriah Travis bought the land from the Commissioners of Forfeiture. See Lederer, *Place Names of Westchester County*, 145.
44. Spear, *To End the War*, 77–78. I disagree with the author's identification of Purdy Hill as the "bald hill."
45. Scharf, *History of Westchester County*, 449.

Chapter 8

46. Martin, *Narrative*, 41
47. In 1776, the river ran farther east than its present course, with Willow Lake situated about where the North White Plains rail yards are today. The lake and river were later relocated westward due to railroad construction. A legendary skirmish later in the war would give Willow Lake the local nickname of "Dead Man's Lake."

Chapter 9

48. Scharf, *History of Westchester County*, 433.
49. Tripoli, "Mount Kisco's Invisible Church."
50. Brace, memorial page for Simon Patch Sr.

Chapter 10

51. The origin of the term is uncertain, but I think this is the most plausible explanation.
52. Hoffman, *Battle of White Plains*, 21.
53. The building is still standing at 49 Lake Street, but I have not found confirmation of this tale.
54. Tomback, *Miller House*.
55. The exact location of Lee's trial is not altogether clear from the surviving accounts, but historian Christian McBurney thinks the Miller house is the most likely location, a choice corroborated by Washington's confirmed location in the Purdy house. See McBurney, *George Washington's Nemesis*, 290–91.
56. McBurney, "Ann Bates."
57. McBride and McBride, "A Family Divided," 25–31.
58. Kennedy, *James Lawless, Jr.*, 93–94. The name was also spelled Chadderdon and Chadderton; see Genealogy.com, "Chadderdon."

Chapter 11

59. McSharry, "Illustrating White Plains History."
60. *Oneonta Daily Star*, "Activities of Real Estate Men Censured," 1.
61. Melvin, "Truce Is Called."

BIBLIOGRAPHY

Books and Publications

Atkinson, Rick. *The British Are Coming: The War for America, Lexington to Princeton, 1775–1777*. New York: Henry Holt and Company, 2019.

Baird, Charles Washington. *History of Rye, Westchester County, New York*. New York: Anson D.F. Randolph & Co., 1871.

Barr, Lockwood. *The Ancient Town of Pelham, Westchester County, State of New York*. Richmond, VA: Dietz Press, 1946.

Billias, George Athan. *General John Glover and His Marblehead Mariners*. New York: Henry Holt and Company, 1960.

Brackbill, Eleanor Phillips. *An Uncommon Cape: Researching the Histories and Mysteries of a Property*. Albany, NY: SUNY Press, 2012.

Buchanan, John. *The Road to Valley Forge: How Washington Built the Army That Won the Revolution*. New York: John Wiley & Sons, 2004.

Collins, Paul E. *Enoch Crosby the Shoemaker Spy*. Conneaut Lake, PA: Page Publishing, 2020.

Countryman, Edward. *A People in Revolution: The American Revolution and Political Society in New York, 1760–1790*. Baltimore, MD: Johns Hopkins University Press, 1981.

Ewald, Johann. *Diary of the American War: A Hessian Journal*. Edited by Joseph P. Tustin. New Haven, CT: Yale University Press, 1979.

Ferling, John. *Almost a Miracle: The American Victory in the War of Independence*. New York: Oxford University Press, 2007.

Fischer, David Hackett. *Washington's Crossing*. New York: Oxford University Press, 2004.

Flavell, Julie. *The Howe Dynasty: The Untold Story of a Military Family and the Women Behind Britain's Wars for America*. New York: Liveright Publishing, 2021.

Gallagher, John J. *The Battle of Brooklyn 1776*. New York: Sharpedon, 1995.

Gara, Donald J. *The Queen's American Rangers*. Yardley, PA: Westholme Publishing, 2015.

Gruber, Ira D. *The Howe Brothers and the American Revolution*. New York: W.W. Norton & Company, 1972.

Hatfield, Abraham. *The Hatfields of Westchester*. New York: New York Genealogical and Biographical Society, 1935.

Henderson, Peter. *Campaign of Chaos…1776: In the Jaws of the Juggernaut an Eaglet Held the Stars*. Haworth, NJ: Archives Ink, 1975.

Hoffman, Renoda. *The Battle of White Plains*. White Plains, NY: Battle of White Plains Monument Committee, n.d.

Hufeland, Otto. *Westchester County during the American Revolution 1775–1783*. White Plains, NY: Westchester County Historical Society, 1926.

Johnston, Henry P. *The Battle of Harlem Heights*. New York: Macmillan, 1897.
―――. *The Campaign of 1776 around New York and Brooklyn*. Brooklyn, NY: Long Island Historical Society, 1878

Kennedy, Ethan James. *Ancestry of James Lawless, Jr*. N.p.: privately printed, 2010.

Kwasny, Mark V. *Washington's Partisan War, 1775–1783*. Kent, OH: Kent State University Press, 1996.

Lederer, Richard M. *The Place Names of Westchester County*. Harrison, NY: Harbor Hill Books, 1978.

Lossing, Benson J. *Pictorial Field Book of the Revolution*. New York: Harper and Brothers, 1860.

Lubrecht, Peter T. *New Jersey Hessians: Truth and Lore in the American Revolution*. Charleston, SC: The History Press, 2016.

Martin, Joseph Plumb. *A Narrative of Some of the Adventures, Dangers and Sufferings of a Revolutionary Soldier*. Hallowell, ME: Glazier, Masters and Co., 1830.

McBurney, Christian. *George Washington's Nemesis: The Outrageous Treason and Unfair Court-Martial of Major General Charles Lee during the Revolutionary War*. El Dorado Hills, CA: Savas Beatie, 2020.

McCullough, David. *1776*. New York: Simon & Schuster, 2005.

McDonald, John MacLean, and William Seymour, eds. *The McDonald Papers*. White Plains, NY: Westchester County Historical Society, 1926–27.

O'Donnell, Patrick K. *The Indispensables: The Diverse Soldier-Mariners Who Shaped the Country, Formed the Navy, and Rowed Washington across the Delaware.* New York: Atlantic Monthly Press, 2021.

———. *Washington's Immortals: The Untold Story of an Elite Regiment Who Changed the Course of the Revolution.* New York: Atlantic Monthly Press, 2016.

O'Shaughnessy, Andrew Jackson. *The Men Who Lost America: British Leadership, the American Revolution, and the Fate of the Empire.* New Haven, CT: Yale University Press, 2013.

Prebble, George H. *Origins and History of the American Flag.* Philadelphia, PA: Nicholas Brown, 1917.

Reno, Linda Davis. *The Maryland 400 in the Battle of Long Island, 1776.* Jefferson, NC: McFarland & Company, 2008.

Rose, Alexander. *Washington's Spies: The Story of America's First Spy Ring.* New York: Bantam Dell, 2006.

Royster, Charles. *A Revolutionary People at War: The Continental Army and American Character, 1775–1783.* New York: W.W. Norton & Company, 1979.

Sanborn, Nathan P. *Gen. John Glover and His Marblehead Regiment in the Revolutionary War.* Marblehead, MA: Marblehead Historical Society, 1903.

Scharf, J. Thomas. *History of Westchester County, New York.* Philadelphia, PA: L.E. Preston and Company, 1886.

Schecter, Barnet. *The Battle for New York: The City at the Heart of the American Revolution.* New York: Walker & Company, 2002.

Smith, David. *Whispers across the Atlantick: General William Howe and the American Revolution.* Oxford, UK: Osprey Publishing, 2017.

Spear, Moncrieff J. *To End the War at White Plains.* Baltimore, MD: American Literary Press, 2002.

Spring, Matthew H. *With Zeal and with Bayonets Only: The British Army on Campaign in North America, 1775–1783.* Norman: University of Oklahoma Press, 2008.

Upham, William P. *Memoir of General John Glover, of Marblehead.* Salem, MA: Essex Institute, 1883.

Valentine, Alan. *Lord Stirling.* New York: Oxford University Press, 1969.

Wertenbaker, Thomas Jefferson. *Father Knickerbocker Rebels: New York City during the Revolution.* New York: Charles Scribner's Sons, 1948.

Articles

Barbieri, Michael. "How Far is 'Musket Shot'? Farther Than You Think." *Journal of the American Revolution*. August 26, 2013. https://allthingsliberty. com/2013/08/how-far-is-musket-shot-farther-than-you-think/.

Bell, Blake. "Cannonball Fired in the Battle of Pelham Found on Plymouth Street in Pelham Manor." *Historic Pelham* (blog). May 18, 2015. http:// historicpelham.blogspot.com/2015/05/cannonball-fired-in-battle-of-pelham.html.

————. "Evidence the Battle of Pelham May Have Begun at Glover's Rock After All." *Historic Pelham* (blog). July 1, 2016. http://historicpelham. blogspot.com/2016/07/evidence-battle-of-pelham-may-have.html

Boyle, Joseph Lee. "The James McMichael Journal, May 27, 1776–October 29, 1776." *Journal of the American Revolution*. February 5, 2018. https:// allthingsliberty.com/2018/02/james-mcmichael-journal-may-27-1776-october-29-1776/.

Burdick, Kim. "Delaware's Colonel John Haslet (1727–1777)." *Journal of the American Revolution*. April 30, 2019. https://allthingsliberty.com/2019/04/delawares-colonel-john-haslet-1727-1777/.

Fanelli, Robert N. "One Famous, One Forgotten: John Eager Howard and Patrick Duffey." *Journal of the American Revolution*. June 8, 2017. https:// allthingsliberty.com/2017/06/john-eager-howard-forgotten-patrick-duffey/.

Geary, Pastor Jeff. "The Gilbert Hatfield House: An Obituary." *Pastor Jeff's Blog*. July 4, 2017. https://revgeary.wordpress.com/2017/07/04/the-gilbert-hatfield-house-an-obituary/.

————. "The Gilbert Hatfield House Part II: Mistakes and Legacy." *Pastor Jeff's Blog*. July 6, 2017. https://revgeary.wordpress.com/2017/07/06/the-gilbert-hatfield-house-part-ii-mistakes-and-legacy/.

Harrington, Hugh T. "The Inaccuracy of Muskets." *Journal of the American Revolution*. July 15, 2013. https://allthingsliberty.com/2013/07/the-inaccuracy-of-muskets/.

Jago, Alicia, Kweku Attafuah-Wadee, Laura Gruenburg, Michael Lueckheide, Michael Naideau, and Justine Paradis. "Rhinebeck's Lost and Found: Free Blacks and the Rhinebeck Association Cemetery, Dutchess County, New York." Research paper, Vassar College, 2011.

Kriss, Gary. "The Rediscovery of Silver Lake." *New York Times*, June 23, 1985.

McBride, Grietje R. (Purdy), and Robert C. McBride. "A Family Divided by the American Revolution: Sergeant Gabriel Purdy UE of the Guides and

Pioneers and Colonel James DeLancey's Regiment." *Loyalist Gazette* 45, no. 1 (Spring 2007): 25–31.

McBurney, Christian M. "Ann Bates: British Spy Extraordinaire." *Journal of the American Revolution*. December 1, 2014. https://allthingsliberty.com/2014/12/ann-bates-british-spy-extraordinaire/.

McSharry, Meghan. "Illustrating White Plains History." *WAG Magazine*, October 2018.

Melvin, Tessa. "A Truce Is Called in Historical Battle." *New York Times*, November 2, 1986.

Oneonta Daily Star. "Activities of Real Estate Men Censured." May 24, 1926, 1.

Poirer, Noel B. "A Legacy of Integration: The African American Citizen-Soldier and the Continental Army." *Army History* 56 (Fall 2002), 16–25.

Powell, William S. "A Connecticut Soldier under Washington: Elisha Bostwick's Memoirs of the First Years of the Revolution." *William and Mary Quarterly* 6, no. 1 (January 1949), 94–107.

Ross, David. "The Hessian Jagerkorps in New York and Pennsylvania 1776–1777." *Journal of the American Revolution*. May 14, 2015. https://allthingsliberty.com/2015/05/the-hessian-jagerkorps-in-new-york-and-pennsylvania-1776-1777/.

Schenawolf, Harry. "Alexander Hamilton the Myth and the Man Part 1: He Never Fired a Shot during the Battle of White Plains!" *Revolutionary War Journal*. January 1, 2018. https://www.revolutionarywarjournal.com/alexander-hamiltons-heroic-role-in-the-battle-of-white-plains-was-a-lie-totally-fabricated-by-hamiltons-son-fooling-countless-historians-and-the-us-government-article-1-of-four-ar/.

Tomback, Sharon. "Miller House in the American Revolution." *North Castle History* 37 (2010), 12–22.

Tripoli, Lori. "Visiting Mount Kisco's Invisible Church." *Bashful Adventurer* (blog). Last updated December 31, 2019. https://bashfuladventurer.com/visiting-mount-kiscos-invisible-church/.

Websites

Diana L. Brace, memorial page for Simon Patch Sr., memorial 24036821, Find a Grave, www.findagrave.com

Genealogy.com. "Chadderdon." www.genealogy.com/forum/surnames/topics/chadderdon.

INDEX

ABOUT THE AUTHOR

A longtime member of the Bronx County Historical Society and the East Bronx History Forum, Stephen Paul DeVillo is a lifelong Bronxite with a deep interest in the history and folklore of New York City and the lower Hudson Valley. For several years, he has developed and led the Bronx River Rambles historical walking tours and has given walks and presentations for a number of other organizations. He is the author of *The Bronx River in History and Folklore* and *The Bowery: The Strange History of New York's Oldest Street*. *The Battle of White Plains* is his third book.

Printed in the USA
CPSIA information can be obtained
at www.ICGtesting.com
LVHW080148221123
764347LV00056B/930

9 781540 252692